Beyond the Moon

an acting manual

by Adam Hill

"I have been

battered and bruised,

praised and lauded.

I have laughed and cried,

fumed and snorted;

I have been <u>beyond the moon</u>

and into the depths of despair.

But in the end,

it has been myself I've had to turn to,

believe in and listen to.

When the time comes,

it is you, and only you,

who knows the truth."

-- Sir Laurence Olivier

You were born with the two most powerful of all acting tools: your imagination, and your belief system.

As a child these tools are evident, and they occupy a great deal of your time. The imagination of the child who plays a game of cowboys and Indians or who has a tea party is soaring. These games are real to the child because they believe them to be real.

Through whatever set of circumstances, these abilities become stifled in most of us as we mature. What needs to be acknowledged is they have only been silenced. It is up to us to awaken them.

Once accomplished, we are on our way to endless creativity.

I dedicate this book to Rosemary Harris.

I'm sure that there have been moments in the past thirty-five years that Rosemary Harris has thought to herself, "What have I done to have this person pop-up periodically in my life?" What she did was to have the most powerful influence on a young actor's life. I may have eventually discovered what she taught me by word and example, but I do know because of her, I learned what I did early in my career, and I am eternally grateful.

She is known to intimates as Rosy. I, however, in all the years I've known her I have been unable to refer to her as anything but Rosemary. Is that because there is something about Rosemary that demands this formality? On the contrary, she is warm, open, friendly, and totally accessible. She is indeed a "Rosy". The formality is strictly mine. I'm sure that she would and does find my hero worship a little awkward.

As a young actor, I was hired to be a journeyman for the renowned APA Repertory Theatre. I was in my final week of training with the Stella Adler method when I decided it would be wise to find out what "auditioning" was all about. I picked up a copy of the trades and in my naiveté auditioned for the first ad I saw. Amazingly I was accepted.

That was the single most important event in my life.

In addition to performing in New York, the APA Repertory Theatre rehearsed and also performed their productions at the University of Michigan, and toured. Not only were we performing one play and rehearsing a second while preparing for a third (Hallelujah!), we also had acting classes that consisted of several different approaches to the craft.

We had speech classes with the renowned Edith Skinner. I did exercises with Keene Curtis, Nancy Marchand and her husband Paul Sparer, Donald Moffot, a host of other brilliant actors, and of course Rosemary Harris.

At the beginning I was too shy to approach her with questions so I just watched. If I did nothing else, that would have been the equivalent of a college education. But I eventually broke my silence and began asking questions. She generously shared some acting exercises developed at RADA, the Royal Academy of Dramatic Arts, where she is now a board member. On one occasion, I had the nerve to ask that impossible of all questions "What is acting?"

She thought for a moment while sitting at her dressing room mirror (I can still see her) and responded, "Acting is dress-up time in Grandma's attic." She didn't explain what she meant and I never asked. I decided she expected me to come to my own conclusion of what she had meant. Throughout the years I've come to realize that what might first appear to be an easy answer, almost flippant (although I've never thought so) was quite wise.

I believe what Rosemary meant that day so long ago is that as actors we need to return to that place where our imaginations, belief systems, and concentration worked in unison to create any world in which we wished to live, and the joy that accompanied that process. (To some that may not be what acting is, but it certainly is what acting should be.)

There are many other moments with Rosemary that have had a profound effect on me. I was having dinner with her in 1996 during the time she was performing the role of Agnes in Edward Albee's *A Delicate Balance*. It was within two months of when the show was to close due to other commitments of the cast. It was an extremely successful production having had a successful run of well over a year. We were joined for dessert by Rosemary's brilliant co-star George Grizzard. These two consummate actors, who could so easily walk through their performances the last two months left in the life of the show, spent their time discussing a moment in the second act that they had an idea of how to improve. All of dessert was a discussion of choices. Those are *my* kind of professionals.

During the time of her Tony award-winning performance as Elenore of Acquataine in *The Lion in Winter* when again we were to meet for dinner between performances. I searched backstage and couldn't find her. Someone suggested I look on stage, which I did while calling out her name. From the house I saw her head pop up from between the rows of theatre seats. I asked her what she had been doing. Her reply was, "I'm cleaning the house for my audience." While walking up the aisle she had noticed some litter left by the cleaning crew…

The ultimate professional.

Editor's Note / Foreword

Non-fiction is more valuable the more it's read and the more deeply it's considered. My advice: don't treat this book as a page-turner; books like this are not trophies to be read and then displayed on your bookshelf as an accomplishment. Read with a purpose. There is much inside this book that will serve you at every stage in your artistic career.

The unique feature of Adam's writing is it's accessibility. If you know Adam, it's impossible not to hear him as you read his words. He speaks and writes in a way that reveals how exciting he finds being an artist, and how passionate he is about his craft. He is devoted to the creative process and to those who are courageous enough to pursue artistic careers. His work is his gift to you.

The first two parts of this book deal with mindset: how you approach your career, and how you understand yourself within it. He starts here, I believe, because he has seen many talented actors fail to enjoy the careers they were capable of having. He feels robbed of their talent. Having been in the industry for 50+ years, he has seen it way too often. Mindset is at least as important as craft. Take the first parts of this book to heart.

Throughout the book, Adam includes quotes from accomplished actors. As a young actor reading this book, you may not know many of the people that he quotes because they are not as popular as they used to be. However, he chose them because their careers have spanned decades. He wants you to model artists who have had lasting careers, not personalities who stumbled into 15 minutes of fame. As study, you would do well to look them up, and watch some of their work.

Personally, preparing this edition has revealed an even deeper understanding. I still learn from his books, even though I've read them many times, use them now for my own students, and have heard him teach for my entire adult life. I hope you develop the same relationship with these teachings as you pursue an artistic career of your own.

That said, if you like what you are reading and want more, if you have further questions or comments, we want you to be in touch. At the end of the book, you can find information on deepening your study with Adam, wherever you are in the world and in your career.

Adam has been my mentor and friend since he talked (maybe *tricked*) me into taking my first acting class in 2000. His guidance and teachings have made a massive impact on all aspects of my life, especially in my concept of myself as an artist. It is an honor and a pleasure to work with him to present his message to you.

Michael Schreiber
September 20, 2013

BEYOND THE MOON

Table of Contents – cont.

Table of Contents – cont.

(article originally written by Adam
Hill for *Pageantry Magazine's* 25th
Anniversary Issue)

INTRODUCTION

What is the craft of acting?

Acting is a set of tools that when combined and utilized in concert, allow the actor to live the life of a character moment by moment, as it is happening, free of premeditation, manipulation or indication.

"Your art is craft."

-- Stephen Sondheim

There is a craft to acting. Learning and perfecting that craft is a lifetime pursuit, as surely as is the dedication required in painting, dancing, singing, or playing a musical instrument.

Acting is easy <u>only</u> when you know your craft. There are no short cuts. There are no magic wands. There is only the need to act and the craft to satisfy that need.

In an interview in American Film Institute Magazine, Robert DeNiro quoted an old acting expression: "In your choice lies your talent. You are only as good as your choices." The craft of acting teaches you how to make those creative choices and then how to make those choices work for you.

The Education of the Sub-Conscious

"Don't try to make things happen... let things happen."

-- Marlon Brando

Why do we study the craft of acting? Acting should be spontaneous! Acting is the product of intuition! Acting is being in the moment! Well, so is driving a car or flying an airplane, but I certainly would not want to be in either with a person who hasn't first studied the craft of driving or flying. Intuition needs to be educated. The more information the sub-conscious has, the better the inspiration. (I can drive a car. However, I wouldn't think of competing with a race car driver.) The sub-conscious is a receptacle containing learned information. There are only two ways information can enter the sub-conscious. It can enter through repetition or, by far the best way, through clear and specific understanding. If I need a surgeon or a dentist or I simply wanted to watch a star athlete perform, I want that person to be a trained professional. When I pay to watch an actor, I want that person to be a trained professional as well.

* * * * *

You can't learn acting from a book. However, you can learn those elements necessary to begin your pursuit of a career, and you can acquire the intellectual knowledge that will enable you to comprehend and grow at a more rapid pace once you have found your ideal place of study.

The search for the right acting school is equivalent to looking for the right mechanic when you do not know the difference between a spark plug and a dipstick. I believe this book will give you a solid understanding of the craft of acting so when you interview for an acting school you will know the right questions to ask and be able to answer any of their questions intelligently.

There is an enormous amount of information in this book. The more times you read it, the more you will comprehend and absorb.

Enjoy and learn.

Part One - Focus – The Successful Energy

"My first job in the theatre was cleaning toilets and pulling the curtain at the La Jolla Playhouse."

-- Dennis Hopper

"You have to give up the life that's planned to discover the life that's waiting for you."

-- Sally Fields

"I'm never actually expecting success, but it doesn't surprise me when it comes, because I know how much work I put into what I do. And I have to in order to complete the fantasy of my life, which is to work at the highest level in the art form that I've chosen to work in."

-- Russell Crowe

"All the good actors I've met have a great respect for their craft. "

--Matt Damon

"I don't believe in pessimism. If something doesn't come up the way you want, forge ahead."

-- Clint Eastwood

"True power is an individual's ability to move from failure to failure with no loss of enthusiasm."

-- Winston Churchill

Who am I? I Am an Actor!

It might appear unwise of a beginning student in the craft of acting to announce he/she is an "actor." Indeed some actors who have spent a lifetime pursuing a craft may find it downright offensive. However, if you don't assert who you are, how committed will you be in perfecting a craft?

Every actor, no matter his or her educational level, experience or how their career appears to be progressing, must name themselves actors. This is easy when we recognize all actors to be "a work in progress."

There are those who consider the profession of acting insignificant, even frivolous. These people, many whom are educated and should know better, can   make those who pursue a career feel uncomfortable, to say the least. Don't allow anyone to minimize your profession. More importantly, don't let them degrade your identity. If you do, you will be allowing them to diminish your dreams.

It isn't anybody's business why you chose your profession. It's only about what you think. If you become uneasy with enquiries, it means you are being uneasy with the essential you. If you become uncomfortable, or if you make excuses for yourself and your career, you will dissipate your drive, energy and motivation.

A Full-Time Job

You will be most vulnerable to negative comments when you are inactive. Doug Savant, a very successful working actor, said one of the most important lesson he learned was **acting is an eight-hour-a-day job**. He was not referring to performance hours. It was the daily work habits of his craft, i.e., mailings, taking classes, reading plays, working on characters, fine tuning his voice and body: the all encompassing work of an actor.

When you work every day at your craft, it becomes much easier to say, "I am an actor." Your paycheck will reflect the amount and quality of work you have invested in your career on a daily basis.

Organize

Organize your days. There is no excuse for avoiding the work you must do to develop your craft and career. It is exhausting listening to actor's excuses. Find a way to do what you have to do!

While I attended acting school in New York City I couldn't afford an apartment, but I wasn't about to give up my classes. I had friends who were interns at St. Vincent's Hospital in New York. The hospital supplied them with apartments. I bunked in with them for an extended period of time. Even the doorman referred to me as Dr. Hill. Although I found a source for free rent which at the time was extremely important there is perhaps a more important reason for mentioning this episode: all that I learned about dedication and hard work while living with these interns. You may call an intern doctor, but he is still a student; he is under the pressure of learning his craft. These men and women worked shifts 72 hours long. No excuses were allowed. I never saw a healthy looking intern in the year I lived there. They all had shallow cheeks and dark circles under their eyes. They put in their time and more. They learned their craft. They set an example for me as to how I should pursue my dreams.

You may say they knew when their training was completed they would be called doctors; they were even being called doctor while interning. If you don't go into your profession with this same assurance, that you are going to be a working professional and be successful at it, then I suggest you find another career. You <u>cannot</u> treat the craft of acting as a hobby. It is a business. And you are a craftsman in that business.

Statistics

We allow fear to influence our approach to our goals. (More on the topic of fear later.) For example, a statistic is that 85 percent, or thereabouts, of SAG-AFTRA and Equity members are unemployed. Consider this possibility: 85 percent are not working because they are choosing not to work. Is this an arrogant thought, an uninformed detail not worthy of consideration? Maybe so, but is it possible that that many people can be unworthy of work? Or possibly some are uniformed as to what is needed to get work and others are downright lazy.

In any case, I personally believe if you are specifically and clearly focused, you will work. The actors I know who work regularly have clear and focused intentions and do what is necessary. If you must identify with a statistic, don't identify with the 85 percent who are not working. Identify with the 15 percent that are.

There is work out there. If one person gets work, it means you can get work. It only takes one job to prove work is available. If you are not getting work while someone else is, investigate why. Don't resort to the excuses: *I'm not pretty enough. I'm not handsome enough. I'm not tall enough. I'm not short enough. I'm not thin enough. I'm not fat enough...* It has nothing to do with your excuses. It has to do with how well you know your craft, how ready you are and most of all how much quality time you are putting into achieving your objectives.

"Play the stakes… why bother playing things that only mean a little to you? I want to get off!"

-- *Alec Baldwin*

Work On Your Career

Working on your career is not about sitting in front of casting directors office's so you can tackle them with your unique form of nonchalant chitchat when they walk through the door. It is not about crashing an "in party" and meeting the director who is going to make you a star. This is about working on your career.

Be informed. Become involved in a support system with fellow actors and share what is happening around town. Read the trade papers. Know who is who and what they are doing. Be informed enough to approach your agent intelligently about being submitted for a role you read about in the trades. (If your agents are not supporting you or submitting you, find the agent who will.) If you want to be seen in an Equity-Waiver production, then go out and audition. Do what is necessary until you begin attaining your goals.

You can sit for hours and bemoan your bad luck. *"I wasn't born wealthy."* Or, *"I don't have a famous mommy and daddy in the business."* The numerous appearances that seem to make someone else's career move simply and swiftly, while your career moves with such difficulty and so damn slow. Well, unfortunately, that's the nature of the game. Doors do open easier for some. However, it's damn hard to keep those doors open, no matter how accurate the above statements are, if you don't have a craft. Besides, it is not about anyone else; it is about what you need to do. Give your attention to what you have, not what you don't have.

Success begins today. It doesn't begin when you pay off your credit cards. If you can't afford a class, then sit in a library and read a play. Talk to people who are successful. Get yourself a healthy support system. Not everything takes money. Form an actor's group and read plays. If you can only find one other willing actor, read scenes together. If you can't find anybody, then read out loud. There's a wonderful adage: *Get off your butt and go to work!*

No Limits

Possibilities for success are astronomical. Consider this: the alphabet has only 26 letters. Yet look how many books have been written and in how many different languages. It's amazing when you consider it. The possibilities are inexhaustible. How can this be true when there are only 26 letters in the alphabet? Does this knowledge stop the playwright from writing his play or the novelist writing her novel? Are they saying, "Look how many books have been written? The chance of me writing something unique is, well . . . there are only 26 letters in the alphabet."

There are no limits. There are only your wants, your needs, your dreams, and the time and hard work you are willing to invest until they are realized.

If you feed your faith, your doubts will starve to death. Remember that this is it. There isn't anything else. Don't procrastinate and deny yourself your dreams. It's a wasteful thing to wake up at 60 and say, *"Why didn't I...If only I had . . ."* (However, it's never too late; our wonderful profession has no age limit.)

The road to success often appears under construction. Because the road is under construction don't wait until the detour sign is taken away. You could easily be waiting for the rest of your life. It's those detours that can keep us vital and alive. Don't allow the construction sites to stop you nor the detours to frustrate you. You don't have any idea what you are going to experience along that new road. It just may be a short cut.

"Be ready."

-- Jack Nicholson

"My career is putting one foot in front of the other. While you hear about others getting brilliant ideas, I simply say, I have to go to work."

Bob Fosse, director/choreographer

There is nothing wrong with brilliant ideas. The more you have the better. Just don't wait around until they come. Go to work.

"Be ready" and *"Go to work."*

Make this your personal slogan.

Commitment

In order for us to realize the depth of our commitment, we must rid ourselves of insecurity and fear. They take many forms. For example, insecurity may be expressed with the question; "Do I have talent?" I don't have an answer to that question. What I do know is that talent is a result of how we have approached the craft. But an accurate definition of talent doesn't exist. Webster defines talent as "a special, natural ability - aptitude." Many "natural abilities" go undiscovered for a variety of reasons. How many now famous performers were once told they had no talent?

"What inspires me is the excellence that DeNiro brings to the work. His respect for the work, the discipline he has about it."

-- Sean Penn

I'll tell you what I believe to be true. Talent is comprised of wonderful instincts that must be expressed and the <u>determination</u> to achieve the goal of that expression. When these elements are combined and married to a craft, a successful result seems inevitable. Ultimately, it is the depth of your instincts that will determine how great you will be at what you do. Not how often you will work, but with what magnitude you will express yourself. I have friends who are superstars and friends who are successful working actors but not superstars. And perhaps someday their instincts will become more powerful and they too will reach superstar status.

There are those who seem to possess more talent... "God's gift." My brother was born with a beautiful singing voice, while I had an adequate one. I cultivated mine. My brother is a motel manager. I've sung on Broadway. In the long run, it's what <u>you</u> do with what <u>you've</u> got.

For example, it is common knowledge and human nature that most people like to look at pretty people. So, pretty people do manage to create an impact in our business. I have yet to know one who has survived over a period of time, though, without learning a craft. A commitment to learning and perfecting a craft will set you apart from actors that believe they can lean on their looks.

It is not enough to want success; you must be committed to it. Those of you who don't commit or who are frightened of commitment will discover you will spend your days continuously using the word "should." Listen to yourself. How often do you say,

I should? *"I should get back into class. I should get Backstage today, see what shows are casting, get a new agent...I should...I should...I should..."* Eliminate "should" from your vocabulary permanently. Commit now!

The life you are living you are living today. You are not dead, waiting to be reborn. You are alive. And the commitments that are to be made are to be made now. Not a moment from now. It's okay that you didn't make them a moment ago: that time doesn't exist anymore. The right time is now.

How to start? If you're standing at the bottom of a staircase, what do you do? You take the first step, then the next step, and so forth.

Nobody is going to do it for you. Let's look at the word *when*. *When* my husband or wife supports me in what I'm doing...*when* my mother says it's all right or *when* my lover says...or *when* my girlfriend and I stop fighting...or *when* my agent, *when* my manager... Nobody but you is in charge of your life. Take responsibility.

Responsibility is the ability to respond. No matter what life has in store, do you have the ability to respond? Do you take action when conflicts occur in your life?

> *"I have a gift for tenacity. I wanted acting bad enough… I went at it. I liken myself to a terrier."*
>
> *-- Paul Newman*

Can avoiding responsibility be less frightening? If I have to be responsible for the life I'm living and something goes wrong, who do I blame? If I am interested in avoiding responsibility, I certainly don't want to blame myself. As a result, I feel that I better not make any decisions, and I go nowhere. Taking responsibility is a much more fruitful path than avoiding it.

I learned a long time ago to remove yet another word from my vocabulary: *blame.* There is no one to blame for anything and that includes yourself. Anytime the word blame sneaks into my belief system, I take special notice and eliminate it as fast as possible. I don't believe it is possible to be a success in life if you're involved in blame. *"They didn't, she didn't, he didn't, why didn't, who didn't, I didn't..."* Failure surfaces many voices. *"That's exactly what my mother said would happen...I'm really not good enough. I should have listened to that teacher. My boyfriend/girlfriend was right. They all said to find another profession. You see, I did it and I failed."*

We are afraid of being proven wrong. The simple fact is there is no wrong. There is no failure. If you approach your career with total commitment and total belief in who you are and what it is you want, <u>you cannot fail.</u> It is impossible to fail. This is who you are. This is what you want.

You are walking down the street and someone assaults you: how would you handle this situation? Are you going to blame that person for what they did to you? Are you going to spend the next few months complaining? *"I was walking down the street doing nothing and this stranger punched me? I don't know why, I was minding my own business?"* Or are you going to take responsibility for this event? What are your options? One is to forget it. It never happened. He did what he had to do. I behaved the way I had to and now it's over. Or a second option: I find this person is a danger and I'm going to do something about it. I will report this person to the authorities.

Something has been done. You have responded. But you haven't dramatized it. You are not making it a soap opera. If a bruise surfaces, put an ice pack on it. Take action. Then it's gone.

There was a time when I needed to blame other people, and I was good at it. After all, those people were out to get me. Even God was out to get me. The devil was surely out to get me. Then I learned the lesson of responsibility. I could control my own life. What a miracle.

Return to your dream. Go back to that wonderful, wonderful child inside of you who expects miracles. Those child-like beliefs will support your commitment.

Believe in miracles. I now believe in miracles because I used to believe in catastrophes. One day, when I got smart, I realized that all the power I invested in catastrophes, I could invest in miracles. I now fill my life with miracles by returning to that child-like innocence and belief I used to have.

There's a poem that reads:

> *We are the dreammakers and we're the makers of dreams,*
>
> *Wandering along lone sea breakers and sitting by desolate streams.*
>
> *World losers and world forsakers, on who the pale moon gleams,*
>
> *Yet we're the makers and breakers of the world forever it seems.*

Why is this true? It is true because you are capable of daydreaming. You're capable of wanting something beyond what the world believes to be practical. If need be, when it comes to your career, be impractical. Remember everyone has a right to bloom where they are planted. Not where someone else thinks they should be planted.

"Concentrated work is a thing of joy unto itself."

-- Uta Hagen

Some of us do not admit to our dreams right away. I have one student who didn't start her career until she was in her late forties. It was always in her heart. And once she realized it, she committed to it and is now a working actress.

My earliest memories were of my profession. And I never allowed that dream inside of me to die. I never allowed anyone to tell me that my dream was not realistic, because it wasn't his or her reality. My dream is my truth.

How <u>much</u> commitment is needed? Sometimes we have to develop a greater commitment because of all the noises in our head. Those voices that might belong to our parents and our friends and our teachers and our critics - those voices that say you can't have. If your commitment needs a firmer foundation, do whatever is necessary. Make it strong and firm. Forge it out of steel.

Here is a story that captures what real commitment is: A man was following a beautiful woman. He followed her for seven days. Eventually she spoke to the man. "Why are you following me?" He replied, "Because you are the most beautiful woman in the world." "I am?" she smiled. "What about that woman behind you?" He turned, looked, and said, "There is no one there." "Ah, true," she replied, "but had you really believed what you said, you would never have turned around."

There is another charming story illustrating commitment. A town in Texas was suffering a severe drought. Everyday the minister would pray for rain. One day he said to the townsfolk, "I think we need more of a community effort. Let's all go to the top of the hill and there we will in unison pray for rain." Only one little girl brought an umbrella.

"I don't particularly respond to the aesthetics of a ballet, but I'm moved by it because of the amount of hours and dedication that went into it."

-- *Sean Penn*

Go into your commitments with belief. Bring your umbrella with you. Don't turn around when someone questions you. Your commitment should be: "I am all that I choose to be in my business." That's it. It is that simple.

Fear

Fear has been described as False Evidence Appearing Real. Fear is a roadblock to the actor. It stops the actor, or anyone for that matter, from getting what he wants. Fears are based on opinions and statistics and ideas. If you want the answer as to whether or not you belong in this profession, ask your heart. And if your heart says yes, allow nothing to stand in the way of your achieving your goal.

"Acting is about courage."

-- *Steven Spielberg*

Fear surfaces all our insecurities. *What if* I'm not good enough? *What if* I never get ahead? *What if* nobody ever hires me?" Here we go, eliminating words again. Scratch out "What if."

15

I'm sure you are aware that no one learns faster than a child? Yet, as the child ages, this rapid growth process slows. Why? Could it be that, as a child gets older, he learns fear? Up to a point, a child is fearless, nothing is impossible. Then that all begins to change. For example, nothing materializes fear in an adolescent faster than the belief he is being ridiculed.

These developed fears in our lives, fear of making fools of ourselves, fear of success or of not succeeding, immobilize us. They do not allow us to grow and fulfill our potential.

Let's uncover a few of our most common fears. *"Am I good enough?"* We spend all too much time processing our feelings of inadequacy and not enough time developing our skills of adequacy. There is nothing to be lost from going forward. Recognize this truth and you will recognize there really is nothing to fear.

If you have a low opinion of yourself as a craftsman, do what is necessary to change that opinion. If you don't know enough, learn more. Put yourself out on the limb. Believe me, there is more pain in never having tried than falling on your face occasionally. Numbness is the result of not trying. Not feeling or experiencing life because you cut yourself off from that which you most want.

Be aware if you fear others and their opinions. Whether it's family and friends or complete strangers, we should not be paralyzed by what other people might be thinking. You know who they are in your life. What power do they have over you?

There is a story involving the painter Rossini. The story begins with his visit to an art gallery. The dealer showed him the paintings of a young artist and Rossini "critiqued" what he saw in a negative way. By chance they came across a few paintings of a different artist and Rossini become enthusiastic. This talent excited him. The paintings turned out to have been painted by the dealer himself forty years earlier. He had quit painting. Why? He had been discouraged by those around him. With tears in his eyes, the art dealer said to Rossini, "Where were you forty years ago when I needed you?"

My feeling is this. Yes, it is wonderful when someone encourages us. The art dealer obviously loved his profession enough by staying in the field. He did become an art dealer. However, if he had listened to his heart, he would have spent his life doing what he most loved, *encouraging himself despite the opinions of others.*

"If you block your unique expression it will never exist and be lost. The world will never have it."

-- *Martha Graham*

Self Worth

There is an old saying: *"There are no victims, there are only volunteers."* A volunteer agrees with what someone is saying about him.

Will you go through life free of fear and anxiety? Of course not. However, as an actor, you know it is impossible to enter onto a stage and do your best work if you have tension in your body that comes from not believing fully in the performance you are about to give. Tension limits the flow of creativity.

This is also true in your day to day living. Having unsupportive beliefs about your ability will stop your growth.

You are worthy. The mere fact that you are reading this book in attempt to improve yourself and your craft is proof of that statement. You are an artist, and you deserve the opportunity to experience your unique creativity, and to share it with the world.

A side note: it is important for you to learn to differentiate between "butterflies," which are energy producing, which get you moving and create excitement, and your enemy: fear, which limits you and closes off your creative juices, creating inertia, creating tension.

Is there such a thing as "beginner's luck?" I don't believe so. What others call "beginners luck" I call naiveté. Beginner's luck is the result of a person who has no fear; a person who walks into situations blindly. Wonderful things occur when we are fearless.

My first few years in the business were full of "luck." I was "lucky" because it never occurred to me that things could go wrong. I had no fear. I had no reason to believe that I didn't deserve to be successful.

"You should never judge yourself."

-- Matt Dillon

To overcome fear, you must let go of it. A butterfly in a cocoon knows that when the time comes to fly, it must let the cocoon go and not drag it around. Let go of the past. Let go of false ideas. Let go of what people think. Let go of statistics. Your only other option is to complain away your life. You can complain that the rose has thorns or celebrate that thorns have roses.

Success is not a station at which we arrive, but rather, it is a way of traveling, that understanding will make a difference. We think of success as the end of the road, instead of knowing it to be the process that leads us down the road. We can fear making mistakes, but if we learn what appear to be mistakes are steps forward, then we can step over them. But if you let them become road blocks, you will never get anywhere.

Perseverance

A man wanted to develop a new soft drink. He was going to name the soft drink "One-Up." He worked and worked on the formula, but it didn't turn out too well. So he decided to make another soft drink and he called it "Two-Up." Again, he worked to perfect it. The result was good, but it really didn't make him feel like he accomplished much. So he worked on another formula and called it "Three-Up." And "Three-Up" was okay, but nobody was really interested when he put it on the market. But he was determined. So he developed "Four-Up" and "Four-Up" was rejected. It was too much like other soft drinks on the market. So he went back to the drawing board and this time he knew he had it right. So he submitted "Five-Up" to the major soda manufacturers. And again he was rejected. So he made another change in his formula and now he was positive of success. He knew that this was the one, he finally had it, and he named it "Six-Up." And once more he was rejected. So he quit.

What can I tell you, I like stories that make my points. The point of this story is we don't know when success is going to happen. All we need to know is that it is going to happen. Until we believe that something is, we believe it is not.

Fear manifests itself when we are unprepared. The answer is very clear. Prepare yourself. Get ready. Eliminate these fears by learning what it is you need to know.

I've been called an optimist my whole life. Is that a bad thing?

There are those who believe an optimist to be someone who approaches each day in ignorance, not knowing where they're going, or how they're going to get there. Here's what I believe an optimist to be: someone who <u>knows</u> what it is he or she wants. Not someone who hopes or prays. An optimist is someone who approaches each day with clear vision. While I believe a pessimist to be someone who doesn't do anything but laugh at the person who is attempting to go places.

Another belief is that by following your dreams you will lose something. What is it that's so valuable you can't afford to lose it? Do you believe your husband or wife will leave if you continue to pursue an acting career? Then my suggestion is let them leave. What kind of life are you going to have with a spouse who will not support you in achieving your goals? It would only build resentment, anger, even hatred and eventually destroy the relationship anyway.

Finally, there is the past. Ralph Waldo Emerson once called the past *"that corpse of memory that you drag along."* What happened to you yesterday, what happened to you twenty, thirty, forty, seventy years ago has nothing to do with you today. If you have to remember the past, remember your successes. Remember when you made people applaud, or laugh, when people wanted and enjoyed being with you. Not the times when you felt embarrassed or when you felt humiliated. Remembering negative times only produces inertia. Remember those times when you were successful and allow those times to support you. You can examine negative experiences for educational reasons, i.e., why did that occur and what can you do so it will never occur again. Examine from the point of growth and not from the point of devastation.

Negatives are destructive. They are debilitating. They create inertia. We end up coping and coping is just another way of not confronting and annihilating our fears. Coping is another way of avoiding what it is that we need to do to get what we want.

Don't verbalize your problems. Don't tell people what is wrong with you, your life, or your business. Talking keeps it alive. The best way to kill negativity is to pay it no attention. Put your attention where it is needed, on your growth. Never give your power away - to anybody or anything. Keep your power for yourself.

Fear of Failure and Fear of Success

We have already touched on these fears, but I'd like to examine them a little further.

Regarding fear of failure, consider this illustration: Most children are aware that before Christmas their presents are hidden somewhere in the house. They proceed to search every nook and cranny and no matter how inventive their parents, the children's persistence keeps them actively on the road of success. The child is so convinced of the existence of presents and the eventuality of opening them that he is void of the fear of not finding them. The unknown is a challenge. The child treats the search as an adventure.

Treat the path to your goal as an adventure. Thrill in the challenge because you are convinced of the eventuality of your success.

Fear of success? I know what you are thinking: you have got to be kidding! Who could be frightened by success? Some of you already know the truth behind this statement. For those who don't, here are a few illustrations:

With success comes an unknown world.

With success comes the maintaining of a degree of excellence.

With success comes the public's awareness of you.

21

And most frightening: with success comes <u>responsibility.</u>

In other words, to be successful, there must be a willingness to experience a certain amount of uncomfortability. Remember it is a part of your nature to grow—neglect this area and you will always experience incompleteness. Looking at your current state of being, is it such that any growth should prove frightening?

In making any major move, the amount of fear you experience depends on:

    1. Your need to make the move

    2. Your preparation

    3. Your expectations

    4. Your inner dialogue

Start affirming the truth about yourself. Here are several examples:

It's time to move. I am no longer satisfied with these conditions.

I have worked hard on my craft. I have enough know-how in order to survive.

I am not a seer; I cannot predict the specifics the future.

I erase the negative voices of the past. This is happening because I am ready and worthy.

Approach your growth with excitement—with butterflies energizing you through your adventure. Your comfort zone will try to talk you out of it. As I said early on, listen to your heart.

Will you maintain your success? Yes, as long as you keep growing! Never have all the answers. But be willing to make having all the answers your goal.

Business Awareness

Learn what is happening in your business. I suggest creating a form utilizing information obtained from the trades or from word of mouth. The form could have fields for Project, Director, Producer, Production Dates, Casting, and Comments.

In no time you will have broadened your knowledge and understanding of your industry. You will be able to communicate intelligently. This awareness allows you to confidently approach your agent. "Have I been submitted?" "Will I be submitted?" If you learn a specific casting director, producer or director you know has a project on board, do not hesitate to drop them a personal reminder mentioning their upcoming project.

Education

Never stop taking classes. You may be sick of classes, tired of doing scenes, tired of sensory work, of improv, tired of your comedy and cold reading classes...

Classes aren't only about acquiring information. Classes are the place to keep your instrument limber, ready and prepared to work.

"I have spent most of my life in the theatre and know that the learning process is never over."

-- Uta Hagen

A dancer would never think of missing class. Even while performing, they still take class. I do not know a vocalist who doesn't vocalize daily. Yet for some reason many actors don't believe they have to. Somehow their instruments are always ready to meet any challenge. It is a foolish belief. Even if you are able to perform a excellent audition without limbering, it still means you are only utilizing a portion of your capabilities.

Never stop growing, stretching and limbering. A newspaper reporter was sent to interview the 92-year-old Picasso. She sat in amazement watching this genius work. "Excuse me," she asked, "but what is it that you're painting?" "Painting?" he replied. "I'm not painting, I'm practicing." He was keeping his wrist limber so that when he approached his work, his hand would flow with ease across the canvas. And so at 92, the greatest artist of the century was *practicing* his craft by limbering his instrument.

"I go back and sit in on scene study classes."

-- *Danny Glover*

Take voice classes and tape your vocal exercises so that every day you can work on them. Have a movement teacher teach you a routine that encompasses all the moves that are vital for an actor. Go through your routine every single day. Work on perfecting your speech.

Do daily relaxation exercises. Repetition of relaxation exercises enables you to eventually control your relaxed state of being. Remember the creative instrument does not work in a tense state. It locks. So it is extremely important to keep your instrument relaxed.

Observation

"Observe and use this great canvas that is out there."

-- Billy Crystal

The following may sound like the most basic of acting lessons to those already in study. It's not to patronize, but rather to remind the professional what he sometimes forgets. And to inform the new actor.

1. Set aside time to watch television and film

Watch a variety of shows, even if for only 10 or 15 minutes. You don't have to be entertained by the show. View it for values, approaches, levels of commitment, and truth. See and note what you like and what you don't like. Observe the differences. For example, in a situation comedy, there are several approaches. One show will play to a very young or teenage audience, while others will be based in physical or external comedy, and others with more sophisticated humor.

2. Read

"It's what attracted me to the theatre in the first place. Shakespeare wrote the best language ever written to this day. There's nothing better, nothing deeper, nothing more complex, nothing more emotional, nothing more, what I like to call, supernatural. It is the finest writing available to an actor."

--Kelsey Grammer

Read a range of plays and read them out loud. Read and watch the classics. You may never do Shakespeare or have a desire to, but the more you open your instrument to the classics, the better your contemporary work will be. When available, rent film versions of Shakespeare, Chekhov, Ibsen, Shaw. Rent the great contemporary plays.

3. Visit Museums and libraries

Wouldn't it be interesting to play a contemporary man with 16th century bawdiness, or a 20th century woman with a 19th century morality? How and where to begin? Visit museums. Read books. Study the clothing in paintings. How did they move in those clothes? Did they stand or sit? Study their attitudes. Look into their eyes. What are they thinking? Proceed to work on what you've discovered. It will develop a sense of character, a sense of place, a sense of event and a sense of another time. Most important you are once again exercising your creative instrument.

4. Visit zoos and other places of interest

Any actor who has ever worked on animals will tell you the enormous benefits of animal exercises. It reveals a world of sensations and behaviors. Study how animals move. Look into their eyes. What are they thinking? Then emulate them. Experience them in your body and thoughts. Again, you're stretching. You're discovering and developing more aspects of your instrument.

5. Watch people

"I find it interesting to watch people thinking."

-- Steven Spielberg

"Watch people... especially watch people under pressure."

-- Billy Crystal

Visit airports and bus stations. Watch people - their emotionality, their "physicality." Study different characters. How do they walk, sit, carry, run, etc? Expand your knowledge. Identify with them. Make notes. And work on your discoveries at home.

6. Listen to music

Discover what music affects you and in what specific ways. Expose yourself to a variety of music. Don't get trapped into listening only to the music you prefer. You're not experiencing the music just because you like it. You're experiencing the music to see how it affects you. If country western music annoys you, or if certain classical pieces make you feel anxious, listen and discover what specifically pushes your buttons. Explore the decibel level on each and see if it enhances what you are experiencing.

7. Watch live theatre

Finally, and most importantly: see plays. Discover which companies around town have a reputation for doing the best plays. Read a variety of reviews. Discover the groups that have the newspapers and trades support. If a classic with a quality cast is performing, make a point to see it. Even if you don't understand what purpose it will serve. I guarantee, in the long run, you will reap enormous benefits. And last but not least, when fellow actors are performing, see their plays. Support them in their efforts.

8. Support groups

Keep in touch with your support group. Share your discoveries, both business-wise and creatively. If you're feeling particularly lazy, call someone in your support group. They may have suggestions that might stimulate your productivity. Don't get caught in pity sessions, though. Remember it's a support system.

We can all too easily indulge ourselves. Don't treat this effort the way most people treat a diet. Do it a couple days and suddenly—*wham!*—the best laid plans go right out the window.

Motivation - Practical Applications

1. Quality time organization

Most of us want to take responsibility for our careers. Allowing this is true for you, re-remind yourself that having a career is a full-time job. If you already have an eight-hour "survival-type" job, then set aside additional quality time for your future. You <u>must</u> put in your time.

Establish a routine utilizing several or all of the following suggestions and reminders. (If my examples spur other creative thoughts, wonderful, the more options the better. Whatever produces the activity that enables you to achieve, do that.)

Set aside a specific time frame for your craft. Don't generalize. If you do, you will find that a week will pass and you'll still be inactive. Your "survival" job, doesn't allow you to come and go as you wish. Let this be true with your career time. Be determined never to vary from the time you've assigned to your craft: That time may be 9 to 5 or 6 to 10 but you must make it consistent. Organize your activities within that time frame. They don't have to be consecutive hours. You may want to spend a lunch hour on one of your other activities. But maintain your daily hourly commitment. Treat your career time with respect.

2. Picture and Resumes

Keep your files and records up to date, i.e., pictures and resumes. Always have plenty available. If your agent has 100 pictures and resumes, you keep an additional 100 in your files. If your agent runs out, he or she won't have to wait while you have more reproduced. Remember, if your agent has nothing to submit, it will be you losing the job. If you are in the process of getting new pictures, be sure to have a few old ones on file until they are ready. If you cannot afford new pictures, remember your current picture is better than no picture. The fastest way to have an agent lose interest in you is to let him believe you are not being responsible for the success of your own career. And one of the best illustrations of irresponsibility is not having your pictures and resumes at hand.

Your resume must always be kept up to date. If you don't have a resume or your resume isn't working for you, consult a resume doctor or your acting teacher. Speak to fellow actors and learn how to construct a resume that will work for you.

3. Mailings and Phone Calls

Keep your mailings current and keep them at a minimum. How to do that? Create a form that contains fields for Casting Director, Production Company, Associates/Assistants, Secretary, Address and Phone Number, and Date Phoned and Mailed. This way you will always know exactly where your mailings stand.

Drop a casting office a card once a month or every three weeks. (just a card, not a full picture and resume, a simple reminder of who you are.) If you are sure that a particular casting director doesn't mind phone calls, (to tell you the truth I don't know if such an animal exist) write down the dates you phone. When calling a casting director, do not <u>insist</u> upon speaking in person. Most secretaries and assistants will relay messages. State as simply as possible who you are and why you called. Then thank them and hang up. Do not prolong the conversation. A successful casting director's office is a busy one and they don't have the time to spend chatting with you. Keep your name in front of them as often as possible without becoming a nuisance.

Create your own audition form with the following information: Date, Producer, Director, Associates/Secretary, Address and Telephone Number, and Comments.

The "Comments" section is so you are able to write down the specifics of your audition. Include how you felt you performed (not "judgmentally" but in terms of what you need to work on to improve your auditions.) Include as much information as you have regarding that particular project. If the casting director doesn't supply it, ask the secretary. Include your impressions of the casting director and what their specific audition requirements were. This form will be invaluable, if and when you have to audition for that particular casting director again.

Belief

There was a time when the world was considered flat and people were limited by that belief system. Columbus believed differently and seeing beyond that limitation, he was able to discover new worlds. Allow your belief in yourself to expand beyond your current belief system. Discover and embrace the world of your future with the conviction of Columbus.

I support you in your growth and the fulfillment of all your dreams.

Part Two - The Unique You

"The responsibility of an artist is to get to know yourself really well and put as much of yourself into your own work."

"A true artist is someone who lets themselves into their own work."

-- *Steven Spielberg*

"Our sensuality, our passion, our sexuality are a part of who we are. It is a part of what makes us walk the way we walk, talk the way we talk, think what we think, go where we go. To take this out of ourselves is to rob ourselves of the part of the fire – the core – that drives us and every character we play. It's the part of me that makes the rose bloom."

-- *Sharon Stone*

"What do you know that you can bring me so I can teach you to act?"

-- *Dennis Hopper*

"Everything I experience becomes a part of my own sense memory."

-- *Danny Glover*

"Your job is to show the world what's beautiful and truthful about life. I go to the theatre to laugh and cry."

-- *Alec Baldwin*

Your Uniqueness

Understand that you are unique. *There is no one like you.* Nobody. The mold <u>was</u> thrown away. You are unique. And it is this uniqueness that is going to get you work. You don't have to look like the reigning superstar. You can look and be exactly who and what you are.

You do not have to look very far to find actors of every type in films and television of any generation.

Consider the film "The Bostonians" (filmed in 1984). It stars five different women: Linda Hunt, Jessica Tandy, Nancy Marchand, Vanessa Redgrave and Madeleine Potter. Here are five actresses starring in the same movie - one was tiny, one was tall, one was elderly, two were middle-aged, one was young, some were plump, some were thin. Each role utilized the uniqueness of these actresses.

There is no one thing you *have to be* in our craft.

> *"Acting is standing up naked and turning around slowly."*
>
> *-- Roalind Russell*

Be your uniqueness. Don't become someone else's idea about whom or what you should be. A young student told me her agent insisted she have glamorous 8x10s. Those photographs received a certain amount of attention. A friend, however, suggested she have one headshot void of make-up. Just being her natural self. She thought, *"What the hell!"* did it, and her work quadrupled. I'm not saying that that's a rule. There are no rules. But it is certainly interesting that when this student presented her own uniqueness, more doors opened.

Your Unique Instrument

"An actor is an instrument."

-- *Paul Newman*

In order to understand your uniqueness, allow me to illustrate in terms of characterization.

Since its conception with all the innumerable performances, there have never been two identical performances of Hamlet. It if were true that there is only one interpretation of Hamlet, all those performances would have been the same. What made them different? The uniqueness of the actor. Every acting instrument is different. There are no two alike.

As an instrument in an orchestra has its own sound, so have you. The trumpet and the violin are two very different instruments. But what the trumpet and the violin can do is play the same piece of music. The result will be each instrument, the trumpet and the violin, will bring its own uniqueness and its own sound to that piece of music.

What is your uniqueness? First, there is no one in the world like you. No one sounds like you, no one looks like you, no one has your creativity, no one has your imagination, and no one has your background or your history. Nobody has the elements needed to create your uniqueness. Yes, there may be others who are similar, but there is no other instrument identical to the instrument that is you. Your job as an actor is to fine-tune this special instrument. Let's begin.

There are four areas of your instrument that need to be fine-tuned:

1. Your physical instrument

2. Your intellectual instrument

3. Your creative instrument

4. Your emotional instrument

Your Physical Instrument

It would be sad not to be able to perform your craft after fine-tuning the other three areas because you don't have control of your body, you don't know how to support your vocal instrument, or your diction is sloppy. More actors unknowingly lose jobs because of ignorance in these very important areas. It's imperative that you take movement classes, whether in dance, exercise class like yoga or sports like karate. Get to know your body. And why should you take voice classes if you don't have any intentions of becoming a singer? An actor must learn control of his vocal instrument in order to support his voice when needed. Speech classes are extremely important. For example, if you have an "s" problem, you may never be cast. Perhaps "never" is too harsh: Humphrey Bogart had an "s" problem and he is still revered to this day. However, for that one who has succeeded, thousands have not.

Is it necessary to change regional accents? Not necessarily. If your diction is good and you support your voice properly, it is not necessary that you rid yourself of an accent. However, be aware that if you do retain an accent, you will be limiting your marketability. In that case, it is then advisable to be accent free. If, however, you feel that you will lose that "specialness" that is you, then by all means maintain the accent. You could also learn the accent of colloquial American. How many English and Australians are now using American accents without losing their own regional sounds?

If you don't know how, learn to relax your body properly. In an audition situation if your body is tense, you will most likely not be considered. It is nobody else's job to make you feel relaxed and comfortable. Yes, it's wonderful when the others makes you feel at ease, but it doesn't happen that often; as a matter of fact, it happens infrequently. You are the professional, so you need to be in control of your body.

If you have physical nervous ticks, such as twitches, biting a lip, twiddling of thumbs, etc., you must be made aware of them, and with time, release them. Anything that stands in the way of your getting jobs or having freedom on stage must be eliminated.

Your Intellectual Instrument

Do you need a formal education to succeed as an actor? No. However, an actor must read, an actor must watch, an actor must listen, and actor must absorb, and actor must be constantly widening his perceptions and understandings. An education is an advantage in acting, as it is in any other profession. Investigate history. What were other ages like? Read historic biographies. Discover how people thought and behaved and what their value systems were. Read current biographies and enlighten yourself to the difference. Most of all - *read plays*. Even if you believe you will never do a play that your future will consist only of TV situation comedy. Read plays. Read the classics as well as contemporary. Expand your understanding.

Expand your thinking. Read books on acting. Look at the different paths other actors have taken. Experiment with what you have read. What works for you and what doesn't? If someone is confiding their problems to you, don't allow yourself to be bored; be attentive and listen. How do they approach their problems? What are their patterns? There is no need to become emotionally involved with all that is going on around you. The task for you is to broaden your awareness.

Your Creative Instrument

"Trust and show that you can trust, so you can make an ass of yourself."

-- *Glenn Close*

In most of us, creativity has always been discouraged. How often has an authority figure said to a child things like: *You're always daydreaming. Get your head out of the clouds. Plant your feet firmly on the ground. Memorize these facts.* There is little encouragement of imagination and creativity outside of kindergarten and the first grade where we are allowed to finger-paint and create with blocks, etc. As we get older, creativity and imagination are sacrificed to the learning of the rudiments of life, how to feed our families and how to pay the rent. That vital side of you, the creative side, has been for the most part, suffocated.

"With any part you play there is a certain amount of yourself. There has to be, otherwise it isn't acting. It's lying."

-- *Johnny Depp*

Give yourself permission to free your creativity to flourish again. It has not disappeared, it has not died. It is still there and vitally alive inside you, waiting for your permission to become active again. At first it may seem that it is not working at full capacity. But with practice and encouragement, it will become what it once was and you will be as excitingly creative as you have ever been.

For those of you who have been blessed by parents and teachers who have encouraged the creativity in you, send a special thank you to these people. You owe them.

(In the Cold Reading chapter, there is an explanation of what creativity is, and how it works.)

Your Emotional Instrument

"If you close down emotionally, then you have to go to work on yourself to find out why."

-- Sally Fields

An actor must be in charge of his emotional instrument. He must be able to call upon his emotional life whenever needed and have it ready to work for him. Here is something every actor should know about their emotional instrument.

Emotions are our friends; they are not our enemies. When we stifle an emotion, we cause problems within ourselves. For example, ulcers and other unhealthy physical reactions are widely understood to be the result of suppressed emotions.

Identification

There is an acting technique, however, that enables us to experience emotions we may not be directly familiar with. This technique is called identification. For example, the rage of a murderer: have you ever torn up a letter when you were angry and/or burned it? At it's core, this is a destructive and murderous feeling, and it may be no different than what a murderer might experience. Thus, we can understand the emotions of murderer by identifying with a destructive moment in our lives.

Now that we have the core of the emotion, you want to intensify it. The process is done exactly the same way, **by identifying what**

you feel passionate about.

It could be a person with whom you are in love. It could be your profession; I know how passionate I am about my craft. It is my first love, my passion. By using this tool I can understand the core of a murderer's rage as well as his passion. I understand it through utilizing an acting technique.

To play a murderer you don't have to be as sick as he is. If you believe you have a sick mind, see a psychiatrist. Acting is not a place for you.

"I went to the Museum of Modern Art every day and would go through the permanent collection doing sensory work...Keep your senses active!"

-- Dennis Hopper

Sense Memory

There are several ways to explore your emotional instrument. The first is sense memory. As far as I'm concerned, there is only one memory and that is sense memory. Let me explain. Our minds (our conscious minds) remember "judgmentally." What remains in memory is the impression an event makes upon us based upon how our judgmental mind wishes to retain it. Two people can experience the same situation, but when they relate what they saw, they will most likely relate two different stories. This is because our minds interpret events as they happen, afterwards translating them to be the way they have impressed us. But sense memory has no little brain attached to it; it does not know how to make a judgment. It only knows the truth of the situation and responds accordingly.

How do I know this is true? For one thing, I don't stick my hand in fire anymore. Somehow, my touch sense memory recorded that I'll get a blister if I do and that it will hurt, so it knows not to do it. When my hand gets near anything that's hot, without thought, my hand immediately retracts.

I have a passion for lasagna. It is even difficult for me to talk about lasagna without salivating. My sense memory is alive with the taste of lasagna and it immediately responds... I salivate.

"Crying is easy... figuring out some other mental things to do is hard."

-- *Shelly Winters*

I smell gardenias and get tears in my eyes. I have even gotten tears in my eyes from the smell of gardenias before I was aware that there was one in the room. Again, my sense memory was at work connecting that smell from a past event in my life. It was my mother's favorite flower and prominent at her funeral.

Sense memory is a powerful acting tool that will always work for you, especially once you learn to trust it. It allows you to become more in control of your emotional instrument. In truth, our sense memory is a combination of our nervous system and subconscious, etc. It is not important that we understand the physiological process that occurs (all information, however, is valuable.) All we need to know is when presented with a stimulant, the physical and emotional instruments react accordingly.

"Sense memory is the best."

-- *Dennis Hopper*

A young actress stated after a class had performed a sense memory exercise she couldn't possibly work this way because she was an instinctive actress. She worked only from her instincts. I don't understand this statement on two levels. There is no such thing as an exclusively instinctive actor because all acting is instinctive, if she is implying that she is being spontaneous. However, when you rely only on your instincts without having done any homework, your instincts will be severely limited.

"At 16 and 17, I did a lot of sense memory."

-- Matt Dillon

To do something instinctively means you can only do it once. If you have to do it a second time, it is no longer instinctive. How do you then recreate it a second time? If you know that you must enter a room in tears, you then must know that you are capable of entering that room in tears as many times as is necessary. If you are doing fifteen takes on a film, you can't turn to the director and say, "I'm sorry. I'm an instinctive actor and unless you get it on the first take, you've lost out." Does that mean that every take is going to be identical? No. Every take will have its uniqueness, although it will be close to the result of what you and your director have agreed upon.

"Of course I resented the people whose instrument was readily available to them. The largest project I had to travel was to find out what made me available."

-- Paul Newman

In all the approaches to the teaching of acting, everyone has his or her vocabulary. When I speak of sense memory, I speak of it as a recreative experience. Simply, the recreating of a sense experience. Let's me explain.

Be aware in your emotional explorations how different sensory experiences have affected you emotionally. There is the old cliché of the *sound* of nails on the blackboard. Do they make you feel uncomfortable or irritable? For most people, the result is a feeling of uncomfortability. What do you experience when you hear the *sound* of a child or a baby laughing? What sensations do you feel when you hear the *sound* of a car braking? Or when you hear the *sound* of a violin playing a specific concerto?

Explore the sense of smell: The different *smells* of ammonia and of lemons; the *smell* of freshly baked bread or brewing coffee; the *smell* of the ocean or the *smell* of sewage; or the potent *smell* of vomit. How do these make you feel? Don't answer in generalities. "this makes me feel good," or, "I don't like it." Be very specific. It makes me feel loving, it makes me feel sad, it makes me feel joyous, it makes me feel calm and peaceful. Explore what these smells do for you.

Continue with touch: The *touch* of fur, the *touch* of sandpaper. For example, two of the most powerful tools you have are heat and cold. How do they make you feel? Also when objects or people touch us what is our emotional response or when we touch the object or person?

Taste: Ice cream melting in your mouth, lasagna (my favorite), sour milk, cough medicine.

You are exploring what are called triggers, buttons or handles to your emotional life.

"I keep my senses open anyway I can. You do whatever you can to keep your senses open."

-- *Dennis Hopper*

Adam Hill

Emotional Recall

The most powerful form of sense memory is what's called a recreative or emotional recall. This is the act of recreating an actual incident from our own life where we experienced an emotion. For example, for that extreme sense of loss, the empty feeling that is beyond sadness, which is the step after grief, I use my mother's death. How do I use it? Do I think about my mother dying? Of course not. As I explained earlier, my mind is judgmental about that. My mind may reject that painful memory and set up barriers. Is this true 100% of the time? No, but one thing I know for sure - rarely will this approach give me what I need as an actor. I choose to go to my sense memory, which I know will work for me 100% of the time if I trust it.

How to use a recreative/emotional recall:

As an actor, you don't have the time to use entire situations to create an emotion. Your job then is to find those triggers that are going to give you the emotions you need immediately. There is a process and it is very simple. In order to discover those triggers, do an emotional recall. By exploring the complete memory you will find the handles for that particular emotion. To explore the emotions I felt as my mother lay in her hospital room - I first must be as relaxed as possible.

Cynics tease about sense memory exercises, "Oh, you have to lay on the floor and do all that kind of stuff." The only reason you lie on the floor is because it is the most relaxed position you can be in. Your emotions flow quickly and easily through a relaxed instrument. They are stopped and blocked by an instrument that is tense. That is why we take the time to lay on the floor. It is not a process of hypnosis nor is it any form of therapy. It's very simply a way to get relaxed. If this position is not comfortable for you, then lean or sit against the wall. But get yourself into a relaxed position.

Accompany your relaxation with deep breathing exercises to rid yourself of any additional tension. Slowly, in your mind's eye, begin to sensorially reconstruct the environment that you were in. Our first sensual area is visual. In your mind's eye, look over to your right and explore what you see there. Don't try to be right. "Well that wasn't there and this wasn't there." That's your intellectual mind getting in the way again, making judgments. Just allow yourself to accept whatever your sensory instrument is telling you. Be aware of colors, shapes, and objects. After you have looked over to your right, repeat the actions to your left. Take your time. See what is there. Continue by looking behind you, above you and beneath you, in that particular order. Always, identify what you see? When something affects you, make the note that you were somehow touched or moved by what you saw. Accept it. Don't make an issue of it.

Remember how you were dressed. How the clothes felt on your body. Next, explore the atmosphere. Was it hot, cold, muggy or dry? How did that affect you? Allow yourself to experience it. Continue with smells. Recognize all the different smells in the room. Don't get hung up on just one smell. Continue with sounds. What were all the sounds? Recognize not only the sounds inside the environment, but also outside the environment. If there were no sounds, what did the silence sound like? If there were no smells, what did the lack of smell smell like? Make mental note of what affects you. Were there any tastes involved? Finally, what was in front of you? If there were other people there, how were they dressed? Look into their eyes. Hear the sounds of their voices. Once you have established all of that, you should be totally involved in the environment and the situation. Now allow the event to unfold. Don't try to feel anything. Allow the stimulus to create the feelings. Discover what were the triggers or handles that created emotions for you.

"What I have available is the whole palette of human emotions. "

-- Danny Glover

I found, as I recreated my mother's death, that I was touched by the whiteness of my environment. This made me feel a specific amount of uncomfortability and fear. The smells were another powerful source for me, that antiseptic smell. This smell made me feel anxious. There was a visual that was extraordinarily powerful; the sight of my mother's eyes as she gazed up at me. But none of them were getting close to the primary emotion I was feeling on that particular evening. The most powerful of all the senses was a touch. I relived the feel of her arm, which was at this point just bone and skin. The arm I used to tease her about. How chubby it was. Now it was hanging flesh and bone. The feel of that arm and the look in her eyes gave me the emotion. It is a source that works for me today with the same intensity it had those many years ago.

"I don't know exactly where I am going to emotionally... all I know is I'm available."

-- Sally Fields

Some may question my using of my mothers deathbed for acting purposes believing it to be inappropriate or rather morbid. It's not. To begin with, the greatest compliment I can possibly pay my mother is by saying to her, "Ma, there is no one else who can possibly make me feel this deeply." By using her death, I am honoring her. No other occurrence has touched me as deeply. As far as morbidity is concerned, remember it is necessary that you have at your fingertips <u>all</u> emotions, because you are going to be called upon sometime in your career to use them. It is not a question of being good or bad or morbid or nice. In acting, it is what is necessary. These are my tools. My emotional instrument is a major tool and I must be in charge of it. I must do the exploring. It is my job.

When I was studying to be an actor, I was the "nicest person" one could ever meet. As a matter of uncomfortable fact, I was nauseatingly nice. The thought of doing and making some of the choices that I knew I had to make was horrendous. It finally dawned on me that if I wanted to be an actor, I had to make not very likable choices. It had nothing to do with being nice. I could be a nice person and yet still make these seemingly un-nice choices. (Finally, I gave up the notion of what a nice person was and began to live my life as a normal human being.)

"Acting is giving something away, handing yourself over to whatever role you play."

--Laurence Olivier

Additional Tools to Activate Your Emotional Life

1. Music

"I use music a lot. I see and hear myself in music terms. I try to find music that helps resonate that music that is in the soul of the character."

-- Jessica Lange

Music is a powerful tool that is very personal to all of us. And, as with any acting choice, you never know the result until you experience it. What is true for one person is not necessarily true for the other. Some of us may be emotionally moved by Chopin and

45

others left cold.

There are several ways we use music. Specific songs will allow us to experience certain emotions. For example, a ballad, such as Frank Sinatra singing *In the Wee Small Hours of the Morning*, may make us feel lonely and set apart. Listening to contemporary music like rap or hip-hop may energize you. For me, a ragtime melody, such as a Scott Joplin tune, makes me feel effervescent and joyful. Many actors, as they are getting prepared in their dressing rooms putting on their makeup and costumes, listen to music that will support them in the atmosphere or emotions they will be experiencing on stage.

There are two other ways in which we use music. We can use music to establish a sense of style or mood for a scene. For example, for the atmosphere of a Restoration comedy, you may choose to use some very lighthearted, harpsichord music. Music can also be used as an energy source. If you lack energy as you prepare for a performance or an audition, choose specific uplifting music. Your low energy will be raised to a high-energy point.

Personally, I am enormously fond of the tool of music. Music has the ability to affect me in both a positive and negative way. I believe that is true for most of us.

Begin to keep a diary of music and the very specific effects it has on you. You never know when you will need it.

2. Psychological gesture

Psychological gesture is an acting tool I consistently use in both performance and audition. What is a psychological gesture? We have, in our bodies, what dancers call "muscle memory." So if I perform a gesture and I do it fully and completely, and then marry that gesture with a thought process, the result will produce an emotion.

Try this: Make a fist. With all your might, start to punch the air in front of you. As you punch it, marry that movement with the thought, "I hate you." And actually speak that thought out loud. "I hate you. I hate you. I am going to get you." You will find if you do this with belief and conviction and you allow your body and your thought to marry, you will begin feeling anger or revenge or whatever emotion is associated with this psychological gesture.

The psychological gesture can be a wonderful energy booster as well. When you feel a lack of energy or a little low or even a lack of self-esteem, and you have an audition or a performance, try this. Bend over, putting the palms of your hands on the floor, with your knees bent. And start to raise to an upright position, dragging your hands over your body, over your legs, your abdomen, your chest, and allow the hands to go above your head and shoot out so they make a total circle and wind up at your sides. In other words, as your hands shoot out, the palm of your right hand shoots to the right and the palm of the left shoot to the left, they circle around your sides and come down with your palms against your legs. As you are doing this, use the thought process, "I am all powerful. I am magnificent. I am the best." Whatever words work for you.

Combine this with oxygen, take deep breaths. In other words, as you are coming up, breathe in and allow the moment when your hands are above your head explosively release the air. You will find if you do this about eight times, you will have more than enough energy to accomplish any goal.

There are psychological gestures for any emotion that you may want to experience in any given scene. Find out what gesture will marry with what thought process to give you the results you need.

3. *As if*

Allow me give a clear definition of "as if" so that it will not be confused with fantasy. An "as if" is a substitution of something I do know for something I don't know. That statement will become clearer as you read on.

To begin with, you can only create from what you know. If I say, it's <u>as</u> <u>if</u> I had a moonbeam in my hand, I would be lying. There is no way I can understand what it would be like to have a moonbeam in my hand. In other words, to use the "as if" of a moonbeam in my hand, I would have to find an "as if" for the "as if." I wonder what a moonbeam might feel like. Well, a moonbeam might feel like cotton candy. In order to understand what a moonbeam would feel like in my hand, it would be <u>as</u> <u>if</u> I was holding cotton candy. I have used my imagination to give something - the moonbeam - a reality through something - cotton candy - I do understand.

"I have great respect for the author and the author's intent."

-- Glenn Close

"As ifs" are very powerful tools. It may be clearer to understand if I define "as if" as a parallel understanding.

Example: A scenario in a film calls for you to be shot. Your job as an actor is to find the tool that will allow you to experience that moment one hundred percent truthfully.

The first thing to do is to find out from an authority exactly what the experience is like. They may explain that being shot is a burning feeling. Can you understand that? It may be explained as a sharp, throbbing pain. Can you understand that? Once you find how you can relate to a gun shot wound, you can get your "as if." A sharp pain? Well, you have been stuck with a needle, you have had a toothache, and you have had a headache. Hot heat. You have burned yourself. You understand these particulars. Now you can deal with creating an "as if" for your wound. It's **as if** a long burning needle were being pushed into my arm.

"As actors, we work from the text! Analyze, breakdown, and then use your imagination...bring your life experiences to a role."

-- Lawrence Fishburne

Use "as ifs" for emotions. If you have never experienced the death of a loved one, it is difficult to comprehend what it would be like. We all have our ideas, but we don't really understand what the emotion is like. How then can you understand that emotion? Maybe at some point in your life someone you loved romantically deserted you. That moment of devastation might be exactly what you need to emotionally understanding the devastation of losing a parent? When you were a kid and your best friend moved away, that was an incredible sense of loss. What you are creating is a parallel understanding.

Can you create from a fantasy parallel understanding? Yes. If the fantasy is strong enough and you have a basic reference point. For example, fear may be created from--and this would work very well for me--a room filled with rats. Or *as if* there were hundreds of spiders crawling up my legs. My basic reference point is one spider or one rat. If, however, I had never experienced a spider or a rat, then it would not work.

4. And the rest...

There are many exercises to help us improve our craft and to make our instrument more alive and vital.

"If you need to be sad, just try hard to be happy, and when you need a belly laugh, try to be still, reverent, and serious."

-- Meryl Streep

Each actor has his strengths and weaknesses. It's important that weaknesses are confronted. Several common areas that many actors need to strengthen: commitment, confrontation, intimacy, vulnerability, releasing, sensuality…

Let me speak a little further about sensuality. When I use the term sensuality, I am not referring only to sexuality, which is most definitely a part of sensuality, but I am speaking of the whole sensual experience. Being vibrantly alive in taste, smell, sound, sight and touch.

It is amazing how unaware we are of the senses we spend our every waking hour with. We don't take time to enjoy and recognize smells, tastes, sounds, textures, and visuals. We live in an immediate gratification world, a world of rushing from here to there, and, unfortunately, or should I say fortunately, this can't be true for the actor.

If you feel you need work in any of the areas mentioned above, don't think in terms of problems. If you do, you probably will feel it necessary to use effort to overcome these "problems." The truth is, these are simply areas that need work. Thinking in terms of problems will create tension in your body, thus preventing you from growing.

Tension creates blockage. That is why it's very important when you work on any of the above areas, you begin the work relaxed.

Part Three - The Foundation

If you are not willing to give what is in the first half of this book a try, what is needed to be a success in this business, you needn't bother to read the second half.

"You <u>have</u> to do the work."

-- Matt Dillon

"When you walk through those doors, you are walking into the theatre. When you walk into the theatre, you are walking into my church. When you walk into my church, you best respect it." (The first words I ever heard in an acting class.)

"In your choice lies your talent." (The second words I ever heard in an acting class)

-- Stella Adler

"What's fascinating about people is what they don't show... they are masters at it. Beginning actors want to show too much."

"I have to love whatever character I'm playing!"

-- Glenn Close

"When a character is well defined, it's up to me to fill in the blanks."

-- Matt Dillon

Acting is Homework

Before defining The Foundation, let's discuss creativity and how it works. All creativity originates in the subconscious mind, which I'll call for this example, our "creative computer." In order for a computer to perform a specific function, it must first have the proper programming. For example, if a computer has been programmed for physics; you would not ask it geography questions.

One thing I know about a computer is that I don't know how it works. I do not know what goes on inside the computer that allows it to compile the information with which it has been programmed and come up with an answer. What I do know is, if a computer has been programmed correctly, it will be able to perform what it is asked to do. Therefore, to request a specific answer from a computer, it must be programmed properly.

The creative computer works exactly the same. Acting is living in a moment. In other words, acting is spontaneous reaction to what is happening around me. Staying within the structure the playwright has created. In order for that spontaneity to occur actors must have stored the information needed in their mental computer.

"Until I found the craft I didn't know how limited I was with these instincts I took such great pride in."

-- Sean Penn

In order for you to be spontaneous in any situation, you must have been programmed to allow spontaneity to happen. So what is programming? Programming is the amount of information you have given your creative computer, that which is stored in your subconscious. It's not what's in your conscious mind. Acting is not a conscious process. **Acting spontaneously and intuitively is the result of homework.**

"Here at The Actors Studio, there is an insistence on the literature of theatre... there is an insistence that you have to use your body and voice, but more than that... there is an insistence that you are immersed in that 7 days a week, 16 hours a day. The people who think they can do it on a two hour class twice a day have not much to look forward to."

-- Paul Newman

The Foundation

The foundation is a series of very specific questions that enable you to explore all areas of the human experience. The more specific you are in creating your foundation, the more specific you will be as an actor. The more specific you are as an actor, the more truthful the life you are creating.

One of the dangers of the foundation is if we look at it only as an intellectual process. It must be an organic or emotional process, as well. I believe the foundation will clarify itself as I go along.

The work has been separated into five different sections. Each section represents a series of questions, a reminder of what constitutes life. When we have answered these questions and breathe life into these answers we have truthfully developed a character living in a situation.

"What is the simple look into the character... where do you start?"

-- Alec Baldwin

The five broad sections I've divided the foundation into are:

1. Who am I?

2. What is my relationship to my environment and the people in it?

3. Given Circumstances

4. Objectives

5. Obstacles

Who am I?

A. Facts

> *"Discover where your character is coming from... In life, you always come from somewhere."*

> *-- Glenn Close*

> *"Find the character's physical center."*

> *-- Danny Glover*

It is very important for us to accumulate as many facts about the character we are to portray as is pertinent. The sources from which we acquire these facts are the script and our imagination. Where the script does not give us the information, it is up to us to fill in the "blanks."

Someone once told me that to be a good actor; you needed to be a good detective. It is up to us to do the investigative work. It is not up to someone else to give us the answers. (When you're working with a talented director this process can become a collaborative venture.) We are always exploring, always discovering new information about our character.

We begin at the simplest level, which is name, age, where we come from, our hobbies, our vocations, our avocation, our education, our current living arrangements, what our family situation is, all historical facts that are pertinent to the development of the character. I always recommend that when an actor approaches this foundation for the first time, he does so about himself. When the actor is finished, the list should represent that actor in a three dimensional way, in other words, the saint as well as the sinner. When working on a character, the actor can use what he wrote about himself as a floor plan.

The actor will note that what originally appeared as random question aren't just random anymore but very specific questions in the development of a character. Write everything down. Why? Its not that this is a test. You are not writing because the teacher told you to. When you write something down, you have made a commitment to what you have written. You write because there will be times you will want to refer back to the information you discovered and the choices you've made. You may want to edit, eliminate, or insert new discoveries. You will find the foundation will never stop growing for you; it will grow and grow and grow.

If you decide to use this foundation, please follow the path I've illustrated. It is the one that I know does work. **The work works.** When you become proficient in your work you can develop your own approach. Until then:

Of all the foundation questions, facts should be the longest, the most detailed. After completing your facts, continuing in the same vein, I would like you to make two columns. Heading one column

"Likes" and the other "Dislikes". Ask yourself random questions. For example, "What is my favorite color?" or "What kind of music do I like?" Make a list as follows:

Likes	Dislikes
the color blue	rude people
classical music	lima beans
cheesy eggs	the sound of car horns

Whatever comes to mind, write down. Make it as varied as possible. You should have at least twenty or twenty-five things on the list. Please do this about yourself first to add to your character's floor plan.

After completing that list, create a second list. Heading one column, "Things I can do" and the other "Things I cannot do." The items on the list can range from very simple things to more unique.

For example:

Things I can do	Things I cannot do
Talk	Fly an airplane
Play the piano	Program computers
Drive a car	Speak fluent French
Cook great French toast	Dance

The column of things you cannot do is not things you are incapable of learning; it simply means things you cannot do at the moment. Usually you will find that dreams creep into this particular category. And it's very important that we discover what quiet, little, subtle dreams our characters may be having. And by first exploring yourself, you will be able to identify those of your characters more easily.

"Part of preparing a character is getting a library of images from that character's life."

-- Glenn Close

Why are these two lists important? Who cares what the character's favorite color is? Whether the character likes lasagna or not? You are programing the creative computer with as much information as possible. I assure you that somewhere along the line, it will manifest itself. Understand it is too easy to fall into the trap of playing one-dimensional characters. These two lists will help guarantee that will never happen.

B. Who am I emotionally?

"My goal: Power, Passion, and Principle."

-- Danny Glover

Compile a list about yourself of between ten and fifteen emotions that express who you are. Not emotions that you are capable of feeling, you are capable of experiencing every emotion, but rather that are a part of your personality. Do not expect to come up with fifteen emotions at once. At this stage of your development you can add to this list what is called, states of being. For example, being nervous is not an emotion; "nervous" is a state of being. But until your emotional vocabulary improves, you can include states of being. Eventually, however, you will understand that nervousness is a result of something else that you are experiencing. You should begin your list with the words: "I am . . ." and then fill in the blank as follows:

I am shy

I am poetic

I am strong

I am vulnerable

I am optimistic

There is no need to go into any heavy explanations or justifications while compiling the list, whether you do this about yourself or a character. Remember, in acting, we are only concerned with specifics; we never deal with generalities or vagueness. If the actor says, *"Well, I am kind of shy except sometimes when..."* that is vague information; it will not be absorbed into the creative computer.

After completing your list, you can express yourself more specifically. Let's say that in your list you recorded, "I am passive." At the bottom you can clarify: "True, I am passive, but if you touch anyone I love, I will attack you." What you've done is made your passivity even more specific.

Making this list about yourself first not only helps the actor by becoming a floor plan that he can look at when starting to work on a character, but it also enables the actor to begin to recognize the uniqueness of his own instrument. This is the instrument you, the actor, will be playing the rest of your life, so know it as well as any violinist knows his Stradivarius. Become comfortable, familiar, and knowledgeable about your emotional instrument. The truth is the average person doesn't need to know himself as specifically as we in the acting profession. Dancers and athletes learn about their muscles, information the layperson need never know; likewise, actors must become knowledgeable about themselves.

Once you learn very specifically who you are, then as an actor you will learn to never play that which you are. This particular statement may seem confusing. Let me express this in physical terms. If you are a blonde and the character you're portraying is a blonde, would you have to do anything? No. Nothing needs to be done. But if the character is a brunette with brown eyes and you are a blonde with blue eyes, then you would have to do something.

The same is true with emotional qualities. If you are already a shy person and the character is shy, you do not have to do anything. When working on a character, you develop only the dissimilarities. If the character is shy and you are not, then you must create shyness.

"Ask yourself, 'What is the emotional journey the character takes?"

-- Jessica Lange

C. Back Story - Character History

The playwright/screenwriter will hopefully supply you with many facts about your characters past. It is your job to fill in the blanks, to use your imagination to create those life experience that are relevant to the events of the play, screenplay, etc. Create those that are needed to make your character more three dimensional.

D. Time of Life

Certain events in our lives can change our personalities, even if just temporarily. For example, if you were living through the slow death of someone you loved deeply, you would begin to carry with you a certain heaviness, a certain sadness, or grief, or anger, or pain. Even if you were at a party laughing and joking, you would still be aware of this heaviness that has become a part of your being.

Even simple incidents can manifest personality changes. Some examples are; when we are in the process of getting ready to move, or those memorable birthdays of turning twenty, thirty, forty, etc. A person who is unhappy in his job will experience personality changes. It doesn't mean the change is forever, but during this particular time, the personality is being influenced by an outside source. Because most plays are about people who are going through some kind of change in their life, it is a very important question and one that must be thoroughly investigated. Again, use your own life as an example.

Environment

"I create an environment to get to the emotion of anger, which is difficult for me, and I don't give a damn who's around me."

-- Holly Hunter

For illustrative purposes, let's say you are the character and your play takes place in your bedroom. The play is entitled, *Getting Ready for a Date.*

A. What is my relationship to my environment?

What is the overall, umbrella feeling of your bedroom? Your room may be your safe haven, your cocoon, the place to escape the world. It may be your think tank.

B. What is my relationship to the people in my environment?

When performing more than likely your character will be on stage with other characters. You must choose very specific feelings/attitudes about each of the people on stage with you, whether you character knows these people or not. (Again, relating to your own life, any person you meet will elicit specific responses from you.)

You develop a relationship with each person that is involved with your character; whether on a superficial level, or on the most intimate level - you must do equal investigations. Of course it is logical that you will have deeper, richer choices the more intimate your character is with the other characters, but don't skimp on your investigation of all relationships.

In the particular bedroom scenario we suggested at the beginning of this section, there is no one else on stage. You are alone in your bedroom getting ready for a date. In this case we have the opportunity to investigate how someone can be on stage with us when they are not physically present. When getting dressed for date, we behave differently depending on whom we are going out with. For example, if it's a business date, the act of getting dressed will be very different than if it's a romantic date. If your date is with someone who makes your heart palpitate, you will behave differently than if that is a blind date that your Aunt Harriet arranged.

Even though a person may not be on stage with you, they will be in your thoughts and/or somehow affecting your behavior. The actor must be very specific about who that person is. What if you never met the person Aunt Harriet has set up, it's a blind date how can you possibly be specific about that person? Because, in your imagination, you will imagine exactly how that person looks, talks, smells, even what their eating habits are. There is no getting around it. You must be specific about your relationships. I cannot emphasize this enough; **if there are magic words in acting, they are specificity and clarity.**

C. What is my relationship to objects in my environment?

Acting is not acting as much as it is reacting. In order for me to react off anything, I must know its value, be it a person or an object. In your bedroom, there are many objects and every object in that room has value. There is nothing that is valueless. Do not confuse the way actors use the word value with the word valuable. It doesn't mean that everything is worth a million dollars. Some things can be worth two cents. There is the paper in your wastepaper basket or that special ring your grandmother gave you. Everything has its value. The actors job is to create that reality for his character.

Everything in an environment must have a value. There will be a set designer and a prop person to dress that environment - but you must be the one who gives it life. No matter how beautiful the set designer makes the set, if you don't make it personal to you, if you don't give it its value, it will not affect you and you will not be able to feed off it, which means you will not be able to react, and that means you will have to start *acting.*

Please do not limit the choices that you make for objects only to the ones that you may speak about or that you have to use within any given scene. Involve every object in the room. It doesn't take long. All it takes is a matter of focus and concentration.

When I'm on stage, if my character has a bookshelf, I can tell you every book that is in that bookshelf. If my character walks into a room that he has never been in before and there is a bookshelf, I, as the actor, will choose what is in that bookshelf. As my character wanders by it, I will know what catches his eye and what doesn't catch his eye and what thoughts he might have about the person who owns these books and how it affects him.

If it is on stage it has a value. If it doesn't have a value for you, get rid of it. If the set designer and the director say it stays, then it's up to you to give it a value. There needs to be a reason for its being there, even if it's ashes in an ashtray. Be specific about not only why it's there but how it affects you. You will find wonderful behavior and a deeper internal life for your character simply by using this particular step.

"I have always been intrigued by these lives I have never experienced."

--Daniel Day Lewis

D. Atmosphere

It is beyond my comprehension how any actor can walk onto stage without creating an atmosphere. The day that I am living in right now happens to be a very hot day in Los Angeles. It affects me. There were people at the door a moment ago, and it affected me. There is noise outside. There is new paint in my environment. I am constantly being affected by what is going on around me. I treat every atmosphere that I live in as an actor with the same value I would if another person was on stage with me - I give it specific attention.

Atmosphere is anything that affects my five senses. Smell, taste, touch, sight, and sound. This can be colors, temperature, noise, or textures. If you are affected by the atmospheres you live in then so is your character.

E. Actual time

Actual time is the investigation of how time affects us and how it affects our character. Time of day, time of year, time of month, time of week. There are people who are incomprehensible at 7:00am. There are other people who, at 7:00 a.m., are ready to conquer the world. There are writers who write creatively at 5:00 a.m. and writers who can only write during the midnight hours. There are people who feel romantic at specific times of the day. There are people who hate winter. There are people who love the spring. There are people who violently object to certain months because of past memories. Time affect us and the exploration of time gives us an opportunity to explore this aspect of our character's life.

F. Historical Time

If an actor is performing a period play, he must acknowledge how that time period affects the life of his character and how his character relates to the time in which he lives.

The top of the list when exploring historical time is the "fashions of the day." Fashion illustrates an historical era. Fashion also affects behavior, the way we think, the way we move, our ideas and our concepts about ourselves.

Another area of exploration is the social and political atmosphere and your character's place in it. Music can reveal a great deal about an era. How affected are you by today's music and fashion? We are going through a health crisis right now and look how that has altered our behavior. We are more health conscious than we were years ago and, as a result, we are more into exercise and nutrition. Fear of terrorists is another thing that is affecting us. If we're responding to the times in which we're living so is our character.

"Bring your (the character's) day on stage with you"

-- *Mike Nichols, director*

Given Circumstances

What were my circumstances before the scene in which I am living and what do I believe they will be after the scene? Let's return to the hypothetical scenario of you getting ready for a date. You might have had a very quiet day up until an hour or so ago when you had an enormous fight with your landlord who insisted you must move out within the next two weeks; and you called your lawyer and had a to-do with him and now you have to get ready for this date.

You can see how your behavior would be very different if you had just won a brand new car. It is important to know from where your character is coming. And I don't mean just physically, but also emotionally. This is the life that you bring into any situation.

The second half of the question is what do I <u>believe</u> will happen afterwards. Your character must live every moment according to what they believe is going to happen. Back to our scenario: you're going out with Aunt Harriet's blind date, which you believe is going to be a horror story. Well, as it turns out, you are going to have the most wonderful evening of your life, but when you were getting ready for the date earlier, you <u>believed </u>it was going to be terrible.

"Always go for what is most interesting, what is most important."

-- Holly Hunter

Objectives

Objectives are the most important aspect in the life of your character. An objective is a goal. It is the thing your character wants. It is impossible to live a moment on stage without an objective for a very simple reason: it is impossible to live a moment of life without an objective.

An objective always takes an active and do-able verb form. All objectives must produce activity whether that activity is on a mental, physical, or emotional level. The more activity, the more interesting the scene will be. Objectives must always propel you forward; they never stop you.

Also, objectives come from the heart. They don't come from the head. It is not something you want intellectually. So when you are seeking an objective, you are doing so according to what your character wants inside, in their gut. This is further intensified by what the character is doing to achieve his goal.

Here are a few rules about objectives. First, an objective is never an emotion. Furthermore, an objective is never a negative. Both emotions and negatives are results of something else. You cannot *do* a result. You can only *show* what a result looks like. For example: here is "happy" - "ha ha ha ha." And you produce a big grin. That is showing what happiness is. But are you experiencing happy? No. Something must happen that will produce happiness.

Remember an objective must produce activity and must always be do-able. That's why it can never be a negative. You all have your pencils positioned and prepared to write. I now give you the objective "to not write". Nothing happens, correct? That is exactly what occurs with all negatives. *Nothing*. Again, in order to produce the result of a negative, you must do something positive.

The following are two negative words: ignore and avoid. In order for me to avoid you, I must be doing something. So if you are sitting next to John and I proceed to have a conversation with him, the result is I will be ignoring you. In other words, for me to do a negative, I must translate that negative into a positive. I must find a way of doing something that produces the result I seek.

"Find the active verb that describes the character or the action in the scene."

-- Paul Newman

Never use the following words in creating an objective: just, maybe, sort of, kind of, try, explain, convince, say, tell, or any word that means talking.

The most important thing to remember about objectives in acting is that they come from the heart. When I was younger, my objective was to become an actor. It wasn't to maybe become an actor, to just be an actor, to convince someone I was an actor, to explain to people I was an actor or to talk about being an actor. My objective, the thing that came from my heart was **to do everything needed be an actor. To accomplish my dream.**"

We must not confuse the different devices or little actions with our objectives. What are actions or devices? There are different ways I took to achieve my objective to become a working actor, different devices. I studied my craft, I got an agent, and I went into summer stock: all of the things that were necessary to fulfill my objective.

These were my devices. Actions and devices are little objectives. (You may call them by whatever name you wish as long as you understand their purpose.)

One area we use actions to the utmost benefit is in our next step, obstacles. We use devices to aid us in achieving our objectives and actions to overcome the obstacles that stand in our way. (Please note: these are just words that enable us to understand the craft. A C-cord in music is still a C-cord no matter what you call it. It won't sound different if you call it a R-cord.)

"You deal with objectives all the time. That's what your drive is... that's your clock, moment to moment objective."

-- *Dennis Hopper*

Obstacles

A. What are my obstacles?

If a shy person wants a job, their objective is to get the job: that is what they want. Their hesitation will be a product of their shyness. If the job is really important to them they will pursue it with an action to overcome their obstacle.

B. What actions do I take to overcome my obstacles?

An action to overcome shyness, as in the case above, might be **to have a prepared speech** or **to look the interviewer directly in the eye** or simply **to take deep breaths**. Without an obstacle and an action to overcome it, there is no play.

Plays consist of three things: objectives and obstacles, with actions to overcome the obstacles. Something you want, something that is preventing you from getting it, and something you do to overcome whatever is in the way. The more objectives and obstacles there are and the more powerful the objectives and obstacles can be, the more interesting the play.

There are three kinds of obstacles:

Physical obstacles. If your objective is **to enter the apartment,** and your obstacle is **you have lost your keys,** you are now dealing with a physical obstacle: the locked door.

Emotional obstacles. For example, you have to give someone you love bad news. Your objective is **to relate the news,** but your obstacle is that **you love the person to whom you must give the news,** or *any* emotion that prevents you from achieving your objectives.

Psychological obstacles. Most psychological objectives or obstacles, however, are emotional in source. But there are a few cases where this isn't true. For example, if you were to play someone who is mentally challenged, you would have to research their illness. One of your discoveries may be that that characters thought process is much slower than yours.

Obstacles can manifest themselves in a very simple way. Actors are very interesting on stage when they allow themselves natural, normal behavior. This consists of tiny obstacles and the accompanying actions to overcome. For example: I itch, I scratch. I'm uncomfortable, I shift in my chair. These are all acceptable theatrical behaviors when they in no way interfere with the focus of the scene.

A Student's Example of a Private Moment

Instead of using a character from a play, I have chosen as my example a student's recreative of five private minutes from her own life. As beginning actors we learn that **if it is true in life it is true in acting, and if it is true in acting it is true in life.** We will make very few mistakes in developing the lives of our characters if we remember that simple phrase.

The student prepared a **Five Minute Recreative**. This is **five private minutes** out of her life on which she based her Foundation. In the future she will use the same procedure in developing her character and the play she is working on.

Who am I? - Facts

"Ask, 'Who are you?'"

-- Jessica Lange

My name is Mary Smith. I am 24 years old. I was born in Colorado Springs, Colorado and raised in Grand Junction, California, where I lived fifteen miles from the small town of Greenbaugh (population 5,000). I have a family of five, two brothers and parents that are still together after 26 years. My youngest brother has Down syndrome, which is a defect in the 21st chromosome. I work as a Loan Processor under a Loan Broker during this decision-making period in my life. I have almost completed college, with just an incomplete to make up. I attended California Baptist College before transferring to California State College at Los Angeles.

I have had a simple life. My parents are both teachers. We went to church every Sunday. I sang solos since I was four years old.

Learned to play piano but never stuck with lessons enough to be any good. I swam on the swim team, played tennis, and was on the volleyball team. I was in the popular crowd but never really thought of it. I was well liked by all the cliques because I didn't place barriers between myself and others. Our school was a mixture of Blacks, Mexicans, Portuguese and Anglo-Saxons.

I was in a car accident when I was a junior in high school in which the driver of my car was killed. I was pretty much responsible for everyone since I was the only one that came out okay; I feel like this has had some kind of impact on my life.

When I was young, I made a decision to be different. I had read the Bible and been a part of the church, but my senior summer, I realized how much truth it had and decided to follow it closely and most importantly to follow the teachings of Jesus Christ. This has a lot to do with who I am; however, I do not judge or place labels on people who do not believe the same way.

I came to Los Angeles to go to a church in East Los Angeles. I worked with high school students in counseling and other areas of their lives. I have been involved in the church, singing, plays, etc. They have a different "mindset." They are friends and supporters.

I spent two summers of my life that were very enjoyable and that I will always remember. I worked for Yosemite National Park one summer, and another I went to India to teach a communication class. I also traveled all over India. I went by myself and although I was lonely at times, it was a challenge.

I have moved eight times in the last four-and-one-half years. I have had a variety of housemates. I had an Australian roommate, lived with a couple and their baby, lived with very emotional people, a couple of preppies, another couple, lived in a dorm, lived with a typical Indian family and visited various other families.

--My critique of her work--

"The more specific, the better the work."

-- Jessica Lange

Critiquing is not about right and wrong. It's about growth. Every critique in acting should be on how to improve on what we have done. I repeat it's not about "right" and "wrong." To begin with, this actress did a good job in developing a **"history"**.

Never stop working on your characters. The day you stop working on your character is the closing night of the play or the wrap party of the film. Up to that time, you are continuously expanding upon your knowledge of the character. Learn this lesson at the the beginning of you career, **you can never know too much**. And this is the problem with this particular "Who am I" – there needs to be more. When playing a character the playwright will give you limited information. It is up to you to fill in the blanks in the characters life and history.

The actress has stated the facts but she is emotionally removed from the facts that she has recorded. Remember in acting, it is not important to know what happened to the character if that knowledge isn't accompanied by how that character was affected by the situation or incident.

For example, this actress states that her younger brother has Down syndrome. But she doesn't state how she felt about that and how it has affected her life. She also refuses to face her deep feeling concerning the car accident. The more in touch with the emotion that surrounds the facts, the more alive it's going to be.

Remember when you do this about yourself for the most part you know what those feelings are. But the next time you do this, it's going to be about a character, and if the character has a brother who has Down syndrome, you will have to know what emotional and psychological impact this has on your character.

The incident of the car accident where everyone was either injured or killed, the only explanation the actress gives is, "I was pretty much responsible and I feel like this has some kind of impact on my life." Those are general statements. What kind of impact? How did it affect her? What were her nightmares, dreams like? How much has it haunted her? What of the guilt that accompanied her feelings of responsibility?

If you are creating a complete human being then you must be able to go into detail on how this character's past has affected his/her life. I am not suggesting the actress needs to explore these questions about herself, but we are using her recreative as an example of how to work on a character. If the character hasn't admitted to the pain that is deep within her we as actors still have to create that pain in order to live the life of that character successfully.

To take this one step further. If any acting teacher forces you to go into dark areas within yourself, don't do it if you are not ready. He is not a trained mental heath expert and has no right in invading your troubled areas. However, if you are an advanced actor, you completely trust your instructor and you feel ready to explore those areas of your emotional instrument you have previously avoided, do so...cautiously.

One of my students mentioned that her mother and father were divorced. That is pretty common. What made it come alive for me was her description of a ten year old girl standing at an airport as she said good-bye to her father. How she watched him get onto an airplane and then watched the plane as it took off and how that separation affected her at that moment. She described the pain and denial that she began to experience. The fact that she was the child of divorced parents became much more vivid. But this is still not enough investigation.

I know you feel that you could write forever. Remember when you are on stage, you are portraying a full and complete, life. You are not portraying twenty percent of that person's life.

"I never give the character less respect than I give my own life."

--Meryl Streep

Who am I – Likes/Dislikes

Likes: Artichokes, pizza, rare steak, kiwi fruit, Indian bananas, to make Chinese food, strawberry crepes, quiche, just cooking for friends and strangers, quiet moments, walking on the beach, looking out a window, the beauty of Yosemite, backpacking, the sunset, the ocean at night, the waves breaking, the feel of water against me as I swim, the feeling after a long workout, playing the piano, singing, intense people, visionary people, wild people, just a close friend, a party, falling in love, getting new things, new clothes, shopping, making someone else feel good, getting to know someone, encouragement, challenges, accomplishments, being on stage, the knots in my stomach, flowers, flowers sent to me, presents, giving presents, wearing sloppy clothes, getting dressed up, doing new things, traveling, eating new foods, trying crazy things, being by myself, being with lots of people, being with just one person, pleasing others, holding hands, watching a movie, escaping, reading a good book, visiting family, vacations, praise, security, financial freedom.

Dislikes: Conflict, being put down, negative sarcasm, falling out of love, nails on the chalkboard, put downs on physically disabled people, put downs on people who are simply different, pet peeves of someone else, trash cans without liners, hair in the drain, getting stains on my clothes, washing dishes, washing my car, dirty clothes on the floor, being late for work, bad haircuts, feeling disorganized, being overweight, comparing myself, beating around the bush.

--Critique--

The "**Likes**" list is wonderful. The actress covers many areas, many diversified likes. Again, I will say it's not enough. When you think you have finally finished put down one more point. In other words, always go a little bit deeper.

"**Dislikes**" is also a wonderful list. However, this list could have incorporated more.

Who am I? – Things I can do and things I cannot do

Things I can do: Sing, play guitar, play piano, play flute, act, swim, play tennis, be a good friend, be a good listener, drive a car, walk, skip, see, hear, feel, love, hate, hold a job, be by myself, travel, live with others, speak Spanish, give a speech, write songs, type, drive a van, drive an Indian car, get along in a foreign country, relate, hope, dare, be challenging, be boring, be in another world, ride a bike, be loved, get around in Los Angeles, use a computer, use a word processor, counsel, be there, write, taste.

Things I cannot do: Scuba dive, surf, rock climb, skydive, speak French, Chinese, Bengali, Italian, German, travel, do things over, take criticism, run out on people.

--Critique--

"Things I Can Do", covers a whole array of areas and situations. Unfortunately, the "Things I Cannot Do" is incomplete. Half of it is covered with foreign languages. You must investigate, dig deep.

Reviewing this actress's "Who am I", my overall comment would be, if this were a character in a play, the character appears to be pretty much one color. I would like to see more diversity.

It is important to discover all sides of our character. If we are playing a negative character, we must find what is positive about our character. And conversely, if we are playing a positive character, we must find the balance in the negatives.

There are no saints. There are no sinners. For those people who appear to be saints or sinners, we must find the different colors in their characters. We must investigate all areas. Even Mother Teresa, and I'm sure she would have agreed, had a dark side to her. (I can only imagine what she would do in order to provide for her sick children.) We are human beings. We have an enormous variety of colors. We must investigate all the possibilities.

Who am I emotionally?

Joyful, lonely, intense, melancholy, ecstatic, happy, sad, unpredictable, passive, impassive, content.

--Critique --

More investigation must be done, what's written here is incomplete. Revealing who you are emotionally is the most difficult of all of the questions you could ask yourself. Only you know how complex you are. This knowledge of yourself should make you explore your characters with more depth. You notice that she chose the words "joyful, ecstatic and happy." While working on a character, I would choose the one word that establishes most clearly what I believe that person is.

There are contradictions - I am happy, I am sad. We are capable of being a happy person and we are capable of being a sad person. But who is feeling the happiness and who is feeling the sadness? Is this a happy person who is feeling sadness or is this a sad person feeling sadness? As you can see, from that statement, the expression of sadness will be different. That is why we have to know who the person is emotionally before we can understand how that emotion will manifest itself.

The actress who wrote this must delve deeper. If this were a character study, her work is incomplete.

What is my time of life?

My time of life is one of change. I am deciding on my future. Do I want to work overseas? Do I want to be an actress? I am in a house situation that is not my ideal. I have been thinking about getting another car. I have gained fifteen pounds in the last six months. I have just ended a relationship that I had hopes for. I have begun to teach children on Wednesday nights. I have just acquired three fish. I am waiting to finish an incomplete for my graduation certificate. I am thinking about getting a Masters in Communications. I have just finished an interview with a Los Angeles Times Magazine writer regarding my household. I am still dealing with my trip to India. I have just finished writing a play in which I had been left by my fiancé. I just decided to drop my Cal State L.A. classes. A relationship with a close friend has not been stable. Another close friend just had a baby. My job is not where I want to be. I am going to make change of life decisions in December before January.

--Critique--

"Time of Life" is actually quite good. She is very specific about the changes going on in her life. Again, what I am missing is how she feels about these changes. Is the future exciting or is it scary? What do these changes mean to her on an emotional level? It always boils down to one question: "How does it make me feel?"

"Never forget the importance of what you do… transporting people."

-- Alec Baldwin

What is my relationship to my environment?

My bedroom is comfortable and makes me feel secure. It is not always private which is irritating. It is a place I don't spend much time in as of late. My roommate is fairly sloppy; I am not the neatest person but her mess frustrates me sometimes. Because the room is so small, there is general sense of disorganization.

--Critique--

The overall feel for the environment is good. However, I am left with only a sense of how she feels regarding her environment. More detail is needed. The following questions may take care of that.

What is my relationship to the people in my environment?

The fish, my only pets right now, the only things dependent on me, are by my bed. Kris, another housemate, is constantly tidying up the place and can be heard outside the door. Holly, my disorganized, intense and unpredictable roommate is not here, buy her strewn clothes, left drinking cups and dirty underwear are everywhere. I always have to leave messages for her because she receives lots of calls. She and I always get along fabulously or terribly. The relationship is bad when she tries to change me to her expectations of what I should be. Or when the mess absolutely overwhelms me. I need to pick up Marie in twenty minutes so I have an awareness of her. I often pick her up from her house and, although she is one of my closest friends, it weighs on me at times. She is an extremely intense person, always on the go, and is even now cutting an album.

--Critique--

As far as the people in the environment, there must be more detail. If someone is mentioned, you must delve into who they are. For example, if my character says he knows Joe and Joe is a good friend of his, and the playwright gives me little information, if I am to talk about Joe, then I must create my history with Joe as well as an understanding of who he is. I must know Joe as well as I know my own closest friends. This is what the actress failed to convey. Many of the specifics she has written should be explored with more depth. Please never feel you have created too many details.

What is my relationship to the objects in my environment?

The bookshelf beside my bed has all the books I am currently planning to read. Some titles are: "Streams by the Sea," "Out on a Limb," "Out on a Broken Limb," "Trauma of Transparency," "Decision Making and the Will of God," "Changes," "Calcutta, City of Joy" (a book I have already read), and "Bengoli Cooking."

The dresser has my jewelry on it, none of which is worth much. My perfumes are also there - White Shoulders, Tea Rose, Chloe, Fake Giorgio, and Obsession. My roommate's Chinese jewelry box overflowing with her junk jewelry is also there.

The carpet on which I am sitting is gray plush and soft to sit on. The calculator I am using I bought before going to India and used when I was there. The pen I took from the desk of my boss and forgot to put back. The checks that have not come in yet and that I am balancing are:

1050 Southern Baptist Credit Union (payment of tax) 28.00

1051 Church on Brady (gift) 52.00

1052 (?) 135.25

1053 Marie (for check she wrote me) 42.06

1054 Sprint (one of two accounts) 16.84

1055 Church on Brady 41.00

My file with all my bills payable and paid is on the floor beside me. Both Holly and I have lots of pillows on the bed, which makes things comfortable.

--Critique--

The objects on the bookshelf near the bed - excellent. Again, I would like to see more investigation as to why these particular books. Otherwise the bookshelf is excellent. Top of the dresser is also good. Again, more detail. (As you see I will continue to repeat this over and over.) The next items are too generalized: more detail is needed as to how she feels about these objects, rather than just a list. Listing of the checks is excellent. Because she is dealing with each check, she must know what each check is and her feelings about them. Overall, this section is not complete.

I understand that to describe every object in a bedroom and the accompanying emotions would entail an enormous amount of writing. But remember, if it is on the stage, you must give it a value. So even if you don't put everything down in this particular instance, you must give full life to every single thing on stage with you. This may seem like a lot of work to you but it takes very little time once you know your character.

Atmosphere

The freeway is not far from our house and I've gotten used to the loud movement of traffic. My fish tank bubbles are a soothing sound, which often puts me to sleep at night. I can hear Kris' cleaning noises. I can smell White Shoulders, which is the perfume I am wearing and I love the soft scent. It is 70 degrees and I am comfortable. The room is done in light colors - white walls with a soft pink hue to the window and doorframe. The curtains are billowy with pink, mauve flowers with different shades of green leaves. There is purple ribbon woven around the flowers. The room has a light feeling despite the stuffiness of disorganization.

"The best way into a scene is sensory work. It's got to come through the senses."

-- Jessica Lange

--Critique--

Atmosphere is marvelous. The room is described but she also writes how this room makes her feel and she includes the senses of sound, sight, smell and touch. Again, a little more detail would only enhance this already excellent description. Of all the environment choices I find atmosphere to be the most powerful. I would never think of entering a playing area without first establishing its atmosphere.

Actual time

It is Sunday, April 26, at 5:06 p.m. Sundays are always a kickback day for me. It feels different than any other day of the week to me. In between 1:00 and 6:00 on Sundays, I feel very relaxed and comfortable. April is the month that has always been just in between. It comes in with a rush and is gone before I even realize it was April. I don't remember many great things from April. A guy I was involved with wanted to get married in April, but I wasn't that interested in him and it was long ago.

--Critique--

Once again the actress has done good work. My only critique is the actress is too casual. There is too much listing of facts without the accompanying emotion. So again, more detail.

Historical Time

There has been a rise in interest rates that will affect my job. The fashion and music of the time is all different. Changing music tastes lean to Jazz and light rock, which I love like Anita Baker. Health - I have just been reading "Fit for Life" and the health craze makes me constantly aware of how unhealthy I am! Also have seen the operation for eyes to have 20/20 vision, which I would consider. A TV evangelist (who I never liked) was just exposed for a sex scandal. Regardless, it had an effect on my life because I am a Christian and some people would want to put me in the same ballpark as TV evangelists and I hate that feeling.

--Critique--

Historical time needs more exploring. When rehearsing a play which takes place in a different time period, you must investigate in order for that time period to be become real to you.

The times we live in affect us dramatically. For example, she states that the fashion and music of the time are different. In what way does she mean? She must be more specific. For example, colors are more predominant in male clothing than ever before in history. The clothes of physical fitness - sweatshirts, sneaker, sweat pants, have become common street ware. All of these things give us a specific idea of a particular era. While some parents think the music of today is sending our children straight to hell the same was said over one hundred years ago by parents about the waltz.

"In order for acting to be instinctual, you have to do a lot of work… you want to get to the point where your imagination takes over… you want your work to surprise you."

-- Matthew Broderick

Given Circumstances

I had been to an interview with my housemates at 12:00 and I am a little worried over how the Los Angeles Times writer will portray us in our living situation. I went over to a group party at a friend's house at 1:30, which was fun, but boring. Five minutes before, I just began working on my checkbook statement. I haven't balanced my checkbook in a while and I want to get it done to see if my budgeting is working out. I plan to be here for another five minutes, but in about twenty minutes I will leave to pick up Marie at church.

--Critique--

The third section, the circumstances before and after, must be explored in more depth. The actress obviously understands all the questions, but she puts a distance between herself and what she is writing. At times I feel she has separated herself from what she is writing. When creating a character, you must explore their passions.

Objectives

Bad time to ask . . . that is exactly what I am dealing with in my life; what are my objectives? For these five minutes I want to get my checkbook balanced so that I will know what my financial condition is. I want to see if I will make it. My budget is extremely tight and I want to be able to pay for everything and be able to take my acting class. I want to get this balanced in a hurry so I won't have to deal with it next week.

--Critique--

On the simplest level, her immediate objective was **to balance her checkbook** and her overall objective was **to maintain her budget (be able to pay her bills.**) Those are her two objectives on the simplest of levels. But remember, when working on a character, it is usually the emotional life that is motivating us and we must look into the character's heart to discover the true objectives in any given scene.

What are my obstacles?

Time is a main one.

Making mistakes on my calculator, having to start all over.

The noises outside my room.

I am tired and moving slowly.

My calculator is solar and needs good light.

Being uncomfortable doing this on the floor.

What actions do I take to overcome my obstacles?

Trying to get it done faster.

Starting over and rechecking for mistakes.

Closing out the noises in my room.

Changing positions to get more comfortable.

Moving my calculator to where it hits the light just right.

--Critique--

Although I'm aware the actress understands this step there are other obstacles that she might have explored. For example, how much money does she have in the bank? How much money does she owe? What are her feelings about these things? There are no emotional obstacles involved. Even if there didn't appear to be any emotional life, if I were playing this character, I would have created emotional obstacles for myself. I want to be emotionally involved in every experience I have on stage.

Overall: For a first try, what this young actress accomplished was excellent. More detail, more specificity and more clarity were needed, but indeed an excellent first try. Remember, the more information you have about your character, the more knowledge you will have absorbed, and the more creativity is going to manifest as you live the life of your character. If your work is complete and specific, the spontaneous life of your character will create wonderful behavior and wonderful inner life.

"Martin Ritt taught me about obstacles. He dared me to see how many balls I could keep in the air."

-- Sally Fields

Part Four - Cold Reading

"I hate auditions, so I turn them into positive experiences... I hold onto my own power."
                                                                    -- Nathan Lane

"I do as much as I can in research and preparation, and then I show up and throw a bunch of things against the wall and see what sticks."
                                                                    --Matt Damon

"Once you've agreed to do a script you must be willing to go as far as it needs to go!"
                                                                    --Ewan McGregor

"Don't worry about right or wrong... I'm not interested."

"Ask yourself, 'Are they picking up the reality that I'm giving them in my reading?'"
                                                                    -- Sydney Pollack
                                                                    (Director, on Auditioning)

"I open myself up every time I walk on screen and give you everything I am. That to me is what my job is."
                                                                    --Kevin Spacey

It's Your Audition

You are in charge of your audition.

If you are looking for work, then you are a professional. If you are a professional, you must be in charge of your audition. Notice how, in your daily life, you are always at your best when you are in charge, when you know what needs to be done.

For example, the first time I tried to hook up my DVD player and my cable at the same time, I nearly lost my mind! (Putting a plug in the wall is heavy-duty electronics for me.) I became a crazy person. I called everyone: the place I bought it, the manufacturers, friends, enemies. I could not fathom what needed to be done and as a result, I went out of control. Since that time, I have learned how to do it and now I am no longer "out of control." Life with my DVD player is easy. Similarly, the actor must become "comfortable" with the audition process so that he no longer feels out of control at his auditions.

How do I become "in charge?"

Learn your craft. That is the first rule. If you believe you can wing it, you're in trouble.

Next is organization. Nothing puts you more in charge than organization. For example, create an audition form. Include the name of the project, the name of the character for which you are reading, the casting director's name and address, the assistant's or secretary's name and a space for comments. This information you can get from your agent. You may also include notes on your performance, including what you wore, in case of being called back at a future time.

When you arrive at the audition, you will meet either a secretary or an assistant. If your agent has not supplied you with their name, introduce yourself, "Hi. I'm John Doe . . . and you are . . .?" They will usually fill in the blank. "I'm Jane or Harry." Use their name and ask for the sides. "Hi, Harry. I've come to pick up the sides for the character of Jim." After receiving the sides, ask for any additional information they might be able to give you regarding the character, story line, the project itself. Unless they are extremely busy, they will most likely impart some information.

If they say, "A story line and character description are written on the sides," you can answer, "Yes, I understand, but can you tell me anything you may have observed; perhaps what the casting director is specifically looking for?" You may also ask if there is a full script available to be read.

Be certain to write down the secretary's name or the assistant's name. Don't forget it. They may very possibly be tomorrow's casting director. Record all information they have given you on your form. Not only will this help you with this particular audition, but your notes will also prove invaluable for future auditions with the same casting director.

Behave as a professional. Find out as much as you can about the project. Read the trades every single day. The more you know about what is happening in the business, the more you will work. Actors who work all the time are the actors who are aware of their business. Be a wonderful and exciting actor, but also be a good businessmen. This work will put you in charge of your auditions.

"Sometimes, in the middle of a scene, I say to myself, 'Breathe'."

-- Danny Glover

The Interview

"Tell me about yourself." Why is this request so uncomfortable? What is it that they want to see and hear when they ask this of you?

One behavior they definitely do <u>not</u> want to see is hesitation or confusion... "Oh... oh... well… let me see... oh… well... I've been... I've been an actor ..." What they want to experience in their office is a professional. The only way you can ensure this is to pre-plan your response. Now this doesn't mean you have a memorized monologue that you intend to deliver. Rather, you have pre-planned various subjects about which to talk, i.e., your training, your first job, an amusing anecdote. If you already know what you are going to talk about, it will flow from of you.

Let it have a beginning, middle and an end. Know exactly what you're saying and be sure to eliminate all the "uhs", "likes", and "you knows". Certain casting directors may say they do not want to hear about your training or your credits or anything that is on your resume. They would rather you small talked. So be prepared for this eventuality as well.

What they are really interested in is your personality. Therefore, if you're going to talk about your training, don't deliver the information factually. Instead, tell it like a story. If you happen to know anything about the background of the casting director and have some similarities to his or her background, be sure to include that and create a conversation.

When you leave their office you want to feel confident that you were in charge.

Intimidation?

"To be an artist, one of the requirements is to risk."

-- *Lawrence Fishburne*

Can an actor be intimidated?

Some casting directors seem to have this ability. There is one in particular who comes to mind. I don't know if this casting director is a mean, ugly person who intimidates deliberately. But I do know actors are, indeed, intimidated by him. And he seems to enjoy it. A secretary or an assistant may try to intimidate you.

Remember that no one can really intimidate you unless you allow them. There is no easy answer to intimidation. We all have our own sensitivity levels.

Here are some suggestions. Don't appear hu mble, angry or lose your composure. Remember that it's your audition. Be very direct with your responses. Following is an example of a possible intimidation:

If a casting director should say:

> What the f*** are you doing here? You're all wrong for the part.

> *(Actual quote from a New York casting director.)*

Do not respond defensively:

> Well, your office saw my picture...

> I came all the way over here...

Oh, I'm sorry, but my agent...

Don't speak to me that way...

Respond, for example:

> I'm sorry to hear that, but as long as I'm here and I'm prepared, I would like you to see my work for possible future consideration.
>
> (You can actually respond anyway you wish but if you want the job these are my suggestions.)

If they respond:

> No, no, I'm too busy...
>
> Do not beat a dead horse. However, if you're going to leave with an emotional hernia, give it one more shot:
>
> It would be important to me.

Remember to be judicious in your choice; if you push too hard, they will simply cut you off before you even begin. Intimidating casting directors are **not** the norm. Most casting people I have met truly like actors and want the best for them.

The Procedure

Don't delude yourself with the belief that memorizing lines is how to work on a script. Don't sit at home and memorize lines. Learn your lines. You do this by having a clear and specific understanding of what your character is saying and why he is saying it. Create the character's truth. **Do your "home" work**, and do your homework the moment you get your sides or the full script if your lucky. It would be to your advantage to don the cloak of your character, and start experiencing that character in terms of his daily life. Take a shower, eat your breakfast as your character, dress with the essence of your character. Become as comfortable as possible in the short period of time you have to work on this material..

"Being in the moment is a very, very, very, very scary place. A very, very, very vulnerable place… you're naked!"

-- Danny Glover

It is the day of your audition and your audition is at 2:00 p.m. If you have a nine to five job, review your homework on the way to your job. Don't overwork the process. Attack your work with a soft touch. Focus your concentration and center yourself continuously throughout the morning. This doesn't mean you cannot perform the duties of your job. But as you do these activities, remain focused and centered. As the time of your audition approaches, put yourself through a good, healthy relaxation exercise. Get your body relaxed. If you are in a place where it's possible to do vocal exercises, do them. Otherwise, do them in your car if you are driving or before you leave the house in the morning. Relax your acting instrument, get everything working smoothly and easily for you. Why? One less worry for you.

Many years ago, there was a pianist on the Tonight Show that impressed me immensely. I was flipping channels and his music make me stop. He was spectacular. Later, when he was finished playing, Johnny Carson asked, (and I paraphrase), "Earlier, when I was passing the studio, I watched you at the piano. The lid of the piano was down and your fingers were traveling up and down the lid. What were you doing?" The pianist told Johnny that he had been doing that for about an hour. When asked why, he replied, "So that when I came out to perform, all I had to do was play. I didn't have to worry about what my fingers were going to do." He got himself ready. Therefore, nothing interfered with his talent manifesting itself. He allowed it to happen. The same reason you want your physical instrument relaxed and your vocal instrument working at peak performance level.

Arrive at your audition early. **Never** arrive late. Time yourself. If your audition is at 3:00 p.m. set your mind for 2:30. No excuses about your busy day or errands you have to run. This is your career. This is your future. This is doing the thing you love to do. This is employment.

I know actors who place more importance on getting to a bank at a certain time to avoid long lines than getting to an audition on time. When you sign in at your audition, check the list and see if they are running on schedule. If they are behind, you don't want to drain you energy by sitting in the waiting room. If you can leave the building. Go for a walk. If there is a coffee shop nearby, visit it. Remove yourself from the audition environment. But stay in character, remain centered.

Gage your return so you have ample time to do your preparatory work. You need to get the life of your character in full swing.

It's your audition time. When you enter the room, know who you are. Know that you are a good actor. Know you can get this role. Walk in with authority. Not arrogance. This is not "I am going to show you" time. Come in knowing the job is yours. You are relaxed and in control. Here is a little trick I use that works well in achieving that sense of authority. Walk as if in a spotlight. Everything else is in shadow and you are in the spotlight.

There seem to be two opinions about the next step. What do you ask after greeting the casting director? One school of thought is that you ask for information about the character. However, I believe that if you have done your homework thoroughly, you shouldn't have to ask this question. Trust your homework.

They may ask if you have any questions. You may tell them you would like them to see the work you've prepared but, afterwards, if they have any adjustments you will be happy to do it again. If they ask if you are ready, say, "Yes I am." Take a moment of preparation. Do not rush yourself but also do not indulge yourself. You should be prepared when you walk into the room. Take a moment to focus, then release and live in the moment.

"Fill up emotionally before your scene."

-- Gene Hackman

Another consideration is dress. Many actors ask the same question, "Should I go dressed as the character?" How much "character" should you bring to the audition situation? You need to use your judgment in each situation. However, let me give you a few guidelines. In most cases, bring in a hint of the character, an aura, an essence. In addition, if the character has an accent for which you are not prepared, do not do it.

When you've finish your audition, make it a rule of thumb that you ask if there are any adjustments that they would like you to make or additional colors they might wish to see. But do this professionally. Never make excuses. If you feel your audition was dreadful, after you leave correct whatever didn't work so that it never happens again.

This is one reason why you list observations after your auditions – observations not only about the audition but also about your work. "I wasn't prepared enough." "I wasn't relaxed enough." "I should have done my vocal exercises." Learn your weak points and strengthen them.

There is only one question I recommend asking a casting director, and only when necessary. Before your audition ask whether he would prefer a theatrical reading or one that is more economical. This is something you will have to ask because they won't tell you. Ask them what type of reading they would like instead of trying to second-guess them.

When your audition is over, leave with authority. Thank them, turn and walk out the door. Don't back toward the door making small talk or chattering. Say, "Thank you very much for your time and making this an enjoyable experience for me." Turn and exit. Also, be certain to thank the secretary or assistant for their help and consideration.

Your audition is now over. This is not the time to brow-beat yourself with "Should ofs." Review your audition and make any pertinent notes for future reference.

The Script

Step One

Read your script for the first time as a piece of entertainment. Enjoy it. **Don't judge the material.** "This is crap!" "This is awful." Treat the material as if written by Shakespeare. Read it with respect. If you are unable to do so, don't do the audition.

Step Two

> *"There is a theme in every work of art."*
>
> *-- Shelley Winters*

Identify all the transitions, major and minor. Usually a major transition affects two people, and a minor transition affects one. However, this is not an absolute rule. You should be able to differentiate the transitions in your script easily. Identify at least two major transitions. The smaller the sides, the fewer transitions there are likely to be. But try to create at least two; transitions bring music to your scene. Besides bringing "musicality" to your script, breaking it down will keep it from overwhelming you. You will focus more clearly. What is on either side of a transition is called a beat.

Step Three

> *"Find the theme of the play and then you ask how do you fit in and how do you fulfill it."*
>
> *-- George Stevens*

The third step is to discover what information the playwright has supplied. When first analyzing a script, don't know too much too soon. If you presume too much at the beginning, then you run the risk of trying to force your choices to fit into your preconceived ideas. Be completely accessible to the script.

A script analysis formula:

1. Pull out the facts as the playwright presents them in the script.

2. Marry the facts and come up with a conclusion.

3. Use your creativity.

For example:

The play: A man enters an elevator on the thirty second floor of his apartment building. He descends to the lobby of the building and asks the doorman to get him a cab. After a few minutes he decides to walk to the corner and take the subway into work.

If I look at the facts and there are many—elevator, thirty second floor, doorman, cab and subway—I can come up with the conclusion my character lives in a big city. Because the playwright used the word elevator I know the big city is not London and because he uses the word subway I know it isn't Paris or for that matter Boston or Washington. In other words, by taking into consideration all the facts, my conclusion will be my character lives in New York City. Now, I can use my creativity and choose my character lives on Park Ave. and Eighty-Fifth Street.

In my example the information seems to be obvious. I deliberately set it up so you could clearly see the process. In most instances, the facts will be more subtle.

Write your facts down. (The actual physical act of writing clarifies your thoughts and also gives you a point of reference when you want to review.) On the day of your audition, use these notes. They will help center you. Make as many notes as possible.

Dialogue contains a multitude of information. From the facts, you will discover who you are and what you want.

For example:

Lila: Momma, let me pick the loveliest roses in the garden!

Lila is a very interesting name - why did the playwright name her Lila?

She calls her mother "momma" - not mother, ma, etc…

Her mother *let* her pick the roses - why? Is she too young? Is her mother strict about the garden, etc…?

Her mother let *her* pick the roses – as opposed to someone else? A sibling?

They were the loveliest - what makes them lovely? Are they different colors, are they buds or in full bloom?

She *picked* the flowers - does this mean choose or physically picked? Did she use scissors, or clippers? Why did the playwright choose roses?

She says *the* garden - not *our* garden. Is the garden hers? Or is it a neighbor's? Perhaps it is her grandparent's?

The sentence ends with an exclamation point.

"You have got to know what the writer is saying."

-- *Shelly Winters*

Once you have written all the facts down, you are ready to "marry the facts." You do this by combining the information you have compiled and making conclusions.

Now you are ready to let your imagination fly. The script will support every choice you make from now on. It will be impossible for you to be "wrong." Since all the information you have gathered is directly from the script, you can only be "right" about your choices - perhaps the casting director will have a different idea about the scene, but armed with all your homework, you will be able to respond to his or her suggestions with ease.

Nine Questions an Actor Must Answer in a Cold Reading

1. Who am I?

2. What am I experiencing emotionally?

3. Where am I coming from?

4. Where am I now?

5. What is my relationship to the other people?

6. What is my objective?

7. What are my obstacles?

8. What action am I taking to overcome my obstacles?

9. What is at risk?

Before we explore each question individually, allow me to make several comments about this approach. If you are a dedicated professional, you already understand the importance of these questions and how vital it is to be specific. Once you have answered each question, you must then develop an emotional/organic understanding of your choices. If your only approach is intellectual, you might as well perform for clairvoyants, as they will be the only ones who will know what you are doing.

1. Who am I?

Using the information you acquired from the script, as well as utilizing your creativity and your imagination, develop a history for your character. Develop a three dimensional personality for your character. Be wary of playing an "attitude" unless that is precisely what the character is doing. For example, if your character is arrogant, find the emotional choice that creates that truth in you. However, if your character is for some reason "playing" arrogant, then you can adopt an arrogant attitude.

Be very careful not to **play yourself** in an audition. If you find the character is very similar to you, leave yourself alone. Just **be.** If the character is charming and you are already charming, if you wind up playing charming on top of that, you will have the casting director in sugar shock. So know your similarities with the character and then leave those alone. It is important that you discover what the dissimilarities are between you and your character. Then focus on those.

2. What Am I Experiencing Emotionally?

Create truthful emotions from all the information you have discovered about the character.

3. Where Am I Coming From?

Where are you coming from both physically and emotionally. Am I coming from a funeral? A birthday party? Be specific. Am I sad? Happy?

4. Where Am I Now?

What environment are you in now? Are you at a ballgame? In front of a fireplace? Is it hot? Noisy? Smelly? Confused? Create your environment as fully as possible.

5. What Is My Relationship To the Other Person?

Do you love them? Hate them? Did you just meet the other person and are in the process of discovery? Do they make you feel powerful? Inadequate? It is your job to react off this person. If you don't know who this person is and what they mean to you how can you react?

"Listening is more important than being listened to. It keeps you fresh, and it keeps you alive."

-- Al Pacino

6. What Is My Objective?

What does your character want? Be more specific here than anywhere else. Some words to avoid when creating your objectives are: *just, try, sort of, kind of, maybe, say, tell, explain, and convince.* These are hesitant, inactive words that, if used, will dissipate the energy of your objectives. (Some acting teachers use the word convince. I don't, but if the word works for you in the audition process please use it.)

7. What Are My Obstacles?

Be certain to create an obstacle of equal value to your objective.

8. What Actions Am I Taking To Overcome My Obstacles?

You must define these for your character. Even if it appears that your character may not overcome the obstacle, you must put forth the effort. Without an obstacle and the action to overcome there is no scene. There are times the obstacle is hidden it is your job to identify the obstacle and use it.

9. What is at risk?

What is at stake? This is the question that can nail the audition. What has the character to lose in this situation?

Example

Objective: To awaken her to my love

Obstacle: She won't listen to me

Actions: To seduce her with the truth

To shake the truth into her

To attract her attention by withdrawing

To wait her out

What is at stake/risk: My live would be empty and desolate without her

The energy of a scene is magnified or depleted depending on our choices. (What you want versus what is stopping you from getting it and finally what actions you are using to overcome your obstacles.) Word choice can be very important here, so it is often useful to have a Thesaurus around to help you choose the most powerful words.

For example, "to savor every syllable she utters" is much stronger than "to listen to what she says."

Part Five - The Study of Acting

"I want to spiritually enhance my life by acting... I want to continually grow as an actor."

-- Holly Hunter

"Uta Hagen's Respect for Acting *is one of my Bibles."*

-- Danny Glover

"Everyone in this business, directors, writers, etc... should study to be an actor first."

"You must take a class in breaking down a script."

"I never stopped studying."

-- Shelly Winters

"I study 4 hours a day, 5 days a week, and spend an equal number of hours away at rehearsals."

-- Sean Penn

"Every actor has to establish a presence that not only fits the overall needs of the story but allows him to interact with the actors in a credible and meaningful way. Every actor wants to work under these conditions and with the material that enables them to create - to use their craft."

-- Toby Maguire

Finding an Acting Teacher

In deciding which acting coach would be best for you, look for someone who teaches the complete craft of acting. Not just one "method." A "method" is an opinion. (Please see "It's All In The Family" for more about the different approaches to the craft.)

Learn as many approaches and acting tools as possible then find the ones that work best for you. You will have developed <u>your own</u> method. For the advanced actor study with the teacher who can help you overcome your weaknesses. For example: If you have problems with your emotional instrument study with a Strasberg teacher. If you have a problem with being in the moment, study with a Meisner teacher, etc.

Respect your teachers, but do not make gurus out of them. Find someone you feel has sensitivity to people and a life awareness. Find someone who teaches with love and not out of anger and resentment.

There are some students who enjoy being berated by their teachers, and I am certainly not going to deny them their means of education, although I personally don't understand that approach to learning. The more your teacher understands the human condition, the more he/she will be able to understand what your particular needs are, and the more he/she will be able to nurture you into becoming the actor that you're destined to be.

Have a teacher who is going to support you. I cringe at the thought of the number of talents that may have been lost due to poor or cruel training. A person doesn't have to pass an exam to become an acting coach; thus, anyone can open an acting school. Unfortunately, some schools are opened by people who, no matter how sincere, cannot teach a craft. Even more unfortunately, or I should say dangerous, is the person who teaches from ego instead of knowledge and love.

Claim the stage you work on in any acting school as your safe place. Know you cannot be hurt by growth. Fall on your face, get up and be brilliant, fall on your face and get up and be twice as brilliant.

"Good live theatre disturbs molecules. You create an energy source around yourself and it alternates between you and the audience. People who see live theatre should come out a little rearranged."

-- Glenn Close

Growing Pains

Those of you who are already trained actors, I'm sure already understand what I'm saying, but for those of you who are beginning your training, let me make clear something about the process of learning the craft of acting or any venture. You will go through periods of knowing and understanding, and periods of confusion. You will go through periods of uncomfortable frustration, or even painful frustration, where you will wonder why you are doing all this. If you are able to survive these moments, then this craft was meant for you.

It's not going to be easy. I don't say this to frighten anyone. All actors go though it. I went through it and it wasn't easy. I literally (yes literally) banged my head against walls when I didn't understand. But I wanted it enough to go through what was necessary to get it. The nature of the learning process is hills and valleys. When we are in the valleys, we will experience these moments of frustration. But when you break through and rise out of those valleys, and you will, you will fly. It is a magnificent, elated feeling.

How can you be assured, after all this study and hard work you will be a good actor? There is no doubt you will be a good actor. I guarantee it. The craft works. If you persist, you will learn. Whether or not you will be a great actor, I don't know. Nor can I guarantee you will be a working actor. That depends totally on you and how much you persevere. There is one additional thing I can guarantee. You will not have wasted one moment of your life. If you are in a good, substantial, healthy acting workshop, studio, classroom, environment, you will exit a richer person.

> *"There is power in the theatre like no place else."*
>
> *-- Glenn Close*

> *"I attend The Actors Studio whenever I can. One must never stop learning."*
>
> *-- Paul Newman*

As for your future studies, there are a lot of young actors who believe that once they have gotten out of acting school, study is over. **Never stop working on your craft. Never stop studying.**

Does that mean you are always going to be in a classroom? If you are fortunate enough to go from job to job, from film to a stage show, to a television show, back to another film, you are working at your craft. Your work will keep you limber. Your instrument is stretching and growing while you are working on different projects with new people and new creative forces around you. If your eyes and ears are open, you will continue to learn and grow and become even more proficient at your craft.

If, however, you go through periods without work, you must return to class. For no other reason than to keep your instrument ready. To keep it limber. I have seen wonderful, brilliant actors who allow their acting muscles to atrophy. Subsequently, when they audition, they are not being cast.

A dancer doesn't stop taking dance classes, a singer doesn't stop vocalizing, an artist doesn't stop sketching, and a pianist doesn't stop doing scales. But for some reason, actors believe they can take long periods of time away from practicing their craft. You are an instrument; you need to be worked.

Why Am I Not Working?

This question is asked by more trained actors than any other. Here, I believe, is the answer. If you are not working, it is because you aren't willing to do what is necessary or you are uninformed as to what is necessary. (The second section of this book: *You Got the Job, is* devoted entirely to this subject.)

Does this answer seem harsh, too simple, or arrogant? If so it is not my intention. My intention is to expose areas where you may lack information and to support those things you already know. Though I will only skim the surface in this chapter, allow me to give a sampling of the necessary ingredients it takes to make a working actor.

1. Organization

Every actor I know who is a successful working actor, is organized. They know what it is they want. They set goals, they research information, and they write their acquired information down!

2. Training

Working actors are well trained and keep their instrument limbered and stretched. They work out as an athlete would by attending workshops and studios on a regular basis when they aren't working, thus becoming **Master Craftsmen**. Your competition consists of many people practicing their craft, but very few **Masters** of their craft.

3. Persistence

Working actors keep working on their careers everyday, even the days that they don't feel like it. They are in daily contact with their agents/managers. They read the trades. They're informed about the business, and therefore, they speak intelligently with those who represent them. They're up to date with their mailings. They are constantly expanding and growing.

4. Support

Working actors surround themselves with positive people. Form a support group. Find a group of actors who are willing to support each other in getting work. (Avoid actors who are always bemoaning their fate. They are debilitating and destructive.) When you hear about a job that you believe would be right for someone, call them and let them know that job is out there. Start supporting others and they'll start supporting you.

5. Keeping Active

Working actors are always working on something. (Makes sense, doesn't it?) Work begets work. Get active in professionally run small theatres if you don't have any other projects at the moment. I emphasize the word "professionally;" research any organization that plans on utilizing your time and talent.

Final Thoughts

All of you who desire an acting career I wish you happiness and success. You have chosen what I consider the most joyous of all professions. I support your total commitment and dedication to your pursuit, as well as the stamina and determination needed for success.

It is, in a way, frustrating writing a book about acting. The learning of acting really is a doing process. It is getting up on your feet, trying, falling down, getting up, and trying again. The nature of the learning of a craft is one of doing.

Take what you've learned in this book. Find yourself a healthy environment to learn and practice a craft.

The profession of acting is a full-time job. If you treat it as a hobby, it will return an equal value. Someone once said about acting that you work eight hours a day just to survive … and then each additional hour is one step closer to guaranteed success.

The mountain climber, in order to reach the summit, must do his research, get his physical, intellectual, psychological instruments ready, surround himself with supportive people, and focus his concentration. In other words, he does whatever is necessary. Then all he needs to do is start climbing. If he persists, no matter how difficult, he will reach the summit. If he gives up along the way, he has made the conscious decision that it just wasn't important enough. At least he knows he gave it 100%. There can be no regrets. Don't wake up late in life with the "If only I had…" blues. Go for it!

"If it can be the other guy, it can be you."

Notes

Notes

IT'S ALL IN THE FAMILY
by Adam Hill

In 1918 Michael Chekhov, nephew of the great playwright, Anton Chekhov, repudiated his mentor and teacher Stanislavsky by debunking his method of training the actor.

In the late thirties the members of the Group Theatre of New York City separated and began teaching the craft of acting according to what each believed to be the best approach; and for the most part debunking the teaching of their former colleagues.

Subsequently, and because of these disagreements, it has become extremely complicated for any young artist wishing to enter this craft to know where or what to study and under whose tutelage.

It would be impossible to display the methods of all the teachers who are expounding theories of acting at present. I have chosen to explore the approaches of several distinguished predecessors, whom I affectionately refer to as "The Great Gurus".

The one thing I ask of you is to read this article through to the end. See if you do not find validity in the teaching of all the Great Gurus.

What follows is addressed to young actors who seek to find specific approaches enabling them to strengthen their individual talents and lessen their specific weaknesses.

* * * * *

Question: What one thing do all the approaches to acting have in common?

Answer: The end result of the actor's homework should be apparent in their performance.

Clarification: That is, they must live the life of their character truthfully, moment by moment as it is happening. They must live the character's life impulsively, with inspiration, and intuition and without manipulation.

In other words, with spontaneity.

Question: Is that <u>all</u> they agreed on?

Answer: No. They all agreed on the Power of the Objective (Lee Strasberg), Action (Stella Adler) or Intention, (Sanford Meisner).

As you can see, there is one thing they didn't agree upon: vocabulary.

Can you imagine learning to play the piano and each teacher you worked with had a different name for adagio or pianissimo or even middle C? Yet throughout the craft of acting there are different words meaning the same thing.

For example: while studying with Stella Adler I was informed that what is on either side of a major transition is called a "step."

In the craft of acting "step" is a wonderful word. I like it because it activates the action that leads me towards my overall objective. Although I teach my students the source of the word "step" and why Stella favored that word, I advise my students to use the word, "beat". Why? Because over the last thirty-five years the majority of those in the industry with whom I have worked use that word.

What is amusing is how the word came to be used in the first place. During the days of the Group Theatre, as the legend goes, a visiting member of the Moscow Art Theatre was asked what he called a portion of a scene. He replied, "Beat!" They said, "What?" He repeated, "Beat!" So they wrote down, BEAT. If his Russian accent hadn't been as thick as it was, we would be calling a "beat" a "bit" for "bit" is what he was saying. I should add that some schools use the words *unit* or *portion*.

Step, beat, unit, portion, bit: These are all good words. There is nothing wrong with any of them. But are they all necessary?

There are many elements of the craft on which the Guru's all agree. What is it then that they discredit in the teaching of others?

The Great Guru's, and Then Some

LEE STRASBERG

Sense memory - Private Moments - Affective Memory

Strasberg describes an actor as one who creates out of himself. (Well, if not out of the self, then where?) This statement sounds good to me. To do this the actor must appeal to the unconscious and the subconscious. The reservoir of our emotions and experience does not lie solely or even mainly in the conscious mind. In order for me to awaken these emotions I must go where they rest: the subconscious mind.

Strasberg believed in the power of sense memory. If an actor recalls certain events in his life and experiences the sensory of the event, these senses will stimulate the body rather than the mind giving the actor greater visceral awareness and experience. I understand this through my own life experiences, as I'm sure you do. How many times I have reacted to a tone of a voice, the smell of a flower or simply extreme weather. There is nothing strange here. I also understand that when I awaken past experiences, certain results become available for me to transfer to the life of my character. My emotions become assessable.

Strasberg believed fervently in private moments. This is an exercise in which an actor lives out a 'private moment' before a classroom audience. As frightening as this may be to a neophyte, acting is about being private in public. By becoming comfortable with being private in public an actor frees his inhibitions. I find this a powerful exercise in achieving this goal.

Here is the big one: Affective Memory. Strasberg says, "The basic idea of affective memory is not emotional recall but that the actor's emotion on stage should never be really real." This confused me until I read further. I couldn't quite believe he meant that emotions should be unreal.

"It should be only remembered emotions," he said.

He is saying one shouldn't experience an out-of-control emotion while performing on stage. Now that makes sense.

It is suggested that by living the emotional life of your character in this fashion it allows that emotional life to vary from performance to performance, yet always remain within the proper framework. (I am paraphrasing Robert Lewis on Affective Memory. If this statement is not entirely congruent with Strasberg's beliefs, blame me.)

While many of the Guru's take a dim view of Affective Memory they find themselves agreeing with Strasberg that work on emotions must not come at the expense of actions (objectives) or characterization.

Strasberg's defenders criticize the debunkers of Affective Memory for their lack of understanding of its true purpose. They assert that Affective Memory is an exercise to be used in practice and rehearsal. It is my belief, however, that Strasberg did not mean for Affective Memory to be practiced during a performance. He was too excellent a teacher and actor to believe it would be possible to split ones concentration like that.

STELLA ADLER

Imagination - Given Circumstances - Characterization - Physical Action.

When I was a beginning student at Stella Adler's I heard the following statements.

"When you walk into this classroom you are walking into the theatre. When you walk into the theatre you are walking into my church. When you walk into my church you had best respect it." Maybe there are theatre people who do not adhere to a religious reference to the theatre but I was taken by this phrase. I have noticed that as the years go by, the actors I hold in high esteem are those who have the most devotion to their craft.

The most resonant statement during that first day of class was: "In your choice lies your talent!" It is hard to believe that most teachers would not agree with this proclamation.

According to Stanislavsky, "The actor needs to act in the circumstances given by the playwright and for heaven's sake there can be no question of feelings at this point." Stella Adler could not agree more with this statement and I believe none of the other Guru's would argue this point.

"The playwright gives you the play, the idea, the style, the conflict the character, etc." Stella was committed to script analysis.

Stella believed that if actors did methodical script analysis, they would be able to translate their findings and arrive at the character the playwright intended. Who can argue with this?

She also concluded that if you live in an imaginary world (the world of the play) it would consist of 99% of your imagination. However, the imagination is based on the facts derived from meticulous script analysis.

She also believed that actors needed to concentrate on the development of their creative imagination. This imagination is crucial, she stressed, to classical drama as well as contemporary. In order for an actor to understand the life of a character within a period or stylized play, they must read, observe paintings, study architecture and listen to music of that time. Who can deny the logic in this way of working?

"In your choice lies your talent!" Stella insisted that if something in the play didn't elicit the requisite end result the actor had to find another set of circumstances that corresponded to the events of the play. Choices that create excitement and internal passion: Personalization!

Stella talks of the "Cold Words!" These are words without understanding, void of any emotional truth. Too often young actors recite lines because they are written on the page. They do not take the extra effort to discover their significance. The words in a play are the source from which we find the hidden lives, the truths of our characters. Stella believed that an actor's inspiration should come from the world of the play.

Stella had immense respect for the written word. Try to get away with paraphrasing Tennessee Williams in a production. She believed as I do (I trust we all do) that the great artist of the written word would prefer not to have their words spoken at all rather than spoken without intellectual, emotional and psychological understanding.

Stella had one statement that confused the hell out of me. "I don't want to see you; I want to see the character." This statement appears to contradict Stanislavsky who said, "Always and forever when you are onstage you must play yourself."

After studying both I came to the conclusion they are equally accurate. Stella did not want to see the boring humdrum life of Adam Hill on stage but the fascinating life of Hamlet. Utilizing *my* emotional instrument, *my* imagination and *my* technique I am able to go beyond myself and become the character. Thus, I am being truthful to Stanislavsky (who went on to say, "You must always be yourself but it will be in an infinite variety of combinations of objectives, and given circumstances which you have prepared for your part, and which have been melted in the furnace of your emotional memory) as well as Stella's' need to see the character.

SANFORD MEISNER

The Reality of Doing - Moment to Moment Behavior

In Meisner's classroom were signs that read: "Act Before You Think", and "An Ounce Of Behavior Is Worth A Pound Of Words". This means, first, get out of your head and then live more than the words. I am simplifying Meisner's message to locate the spirit of what he is saying. Clear basic acting truth.

Active Behavior - Active behavior means that if your character is reading a book in a play, then really read. If he is pacing the room, really pace the room. If you are pursuing an objective **really** pursue the objective.

Sanford Meisner believed there were three parts to the acting process.

Homework

Rehearsal

Performance

The first two support the third. The actor does his homework. Script analysis, emotional work, etc.

The actor then brings the results of his homework to the rehearsal. There he begins to shape his role using the guidelines set by the director. It is during the rehearsal process the actor releases intellectual control and allows the spontaneous instrument to take over.

The performance is the spontaneous, in the moment, living out of the character's destiny.

What in fact places Meisner apart from other teachers are two of his most powerful exercises.

The Repetition Exercise - a valuable exercise for the development of communicative skills. It strengthens the ability to be in the moment and to react off that moment without intellectual interference.

The Knock On The Door Exercise - emphasizes the importance of urgency and the power of circumstances.

This exercise also upholds the importance of preparation and the use of the imagination in the creation of an emotional life.

Is it possible to object to these two exercises?

Stanislavsky states in 'An Actor Prepares', "what an actor needs is a super objective which is in harmony with the intentions of the playwright and at the same time arouses a response in the soul of the actor. That means we must search for it not only in the play but also in the actors themselves."

While I do not presume to put words into the mouth of Sanford Meisner, in all my studies of the Meisner approach, I can't imagine his disagreeing with that statement.

UTA HAGEN

Respect for Acting

"We all have passionate beliefs and opinions about the art of acting. I have spent most of my life in the theatre and know that the learning process is never over."

- Uta Hagen

Both of Uta Hagen's books are required reading in my classes. What I appreciate most in Miss Hagen's teaching is her belief that every one eventually finds his/her own "method" in acting.

She speaks of the legends she has either worked with, knew personally or studied. When these actors were asked about their method, they said they didn't have one. Yet all were meticulous and painstaking in their approach to the craft they practiced. It was from their example and those of the directors she worked with, primarily Harold Clurman (who along with director Elia Kazan has had as great an influence on the training methods of young actors as any teacher), and finally her husband, the great teacher Herbert Berghof, that she established her method.

There are those who approach the homework through the five W's: Who, Where, What, When, Why. Miss Hagen uses nine questions as the foundation for the actor's homework:

> *Who am I?*
> *What time is it?*
> *Where am I?*
> *What surrounds me?*
> *What are my given circumstances?*
> *What is my relationship?*
> *What do I want?*
> *What's in my way?*
> *What do I do to get what I want?*

All Miss Hagen has done is to make the five W questions more specific.I have taken her questions and made them even more specific for myself. Neither my way nor Miss Hagen's way negates the original five W's or any other teacher's method to get to the same results.

MICHEAL CHEKHOV

The Higher Ego - Psychological Gesture - Atmosphere

From 1912 to 1918 Michael Chekhov developed his acting skills in the basic elements of the Stanislavsky method: relaxation, concentration, naïveté, imagination, communication and effective memory. By 1918 he had become a successful actor. He had also become a heavy drinker. The rest of his life at that time was falling apart. His wife left him taking their daughter with her and then his mother died. Just as things seemed hopeless in his life Chekhov discovered a spiritual science called anthroposophy. It's founder's theories (Rudolf Steiner) would have a significant impact on Chekhov's personal and creative life.

One aspect of Steiner's teaching in particular had an intense impact on him. Steiner called it "the higher ego." He interpreted this as the "artist in us that stands behind all our creative processes."

Chekhov identified four ways in which sensitivity to this higher ego would enrich the actor.

> It was the source of the actor's creative individuality.

> It possessed an ethical sense, which enabled the actor to feel the conflict between good and evil in the play.

> It enabled sensitivity to the audience's perspective on a play during performance.

> It brought a sense of detachment, compassion, and humor into the actor's work by being freed of the 'narrow selfish ego.'

I do not believe his mentor Stanislavsky would have argued the importance of these points. The source of creativity and the sensitivity to which it is leading you to an experience during a performance is as critical to the finished product as any of the acting tools being taught by others.

One of Chekhov's great gifts to the craft of acting was the *Psychological Gesture* - the combining of a physical movement with a thought process that brings about an inner emotional response. As an actor I would never go on stage without this amazing tool. Because of its private nature to me, the actor, in my connection to the character, it works as a fuse to all my other choices as soon as I put it to work.

I use psychological gesture both as an actor and teacher. I have made it my own. I didn't learn it from the master himself but from one of his immediate disciples who may have improved upon Chekhov. All I know is, as I understand it, it works for me and I am thankful I have it in my tool kit.

Like Stella Adler, Michael Chekhov focuses on imagination and concentration.

Another point of concentration in the Chekhov approach was atmosphere. Chekhov was more aware of the importance of atmosphere than anyone else at his time, and it became a major element in his technique.

Atmosphere is one of my favorite tools as an actor. While acting in a show I would arrive at the theatre ahead of my fellow actors. I would go directly to the empty stage. There I would spend ten or fifteen minutes creating the different atmospheres for my character to live in. During the performance when it came time for my entrances, the atmosphere I had created earlier would always be there for me to walk into.

THE ROYAL ACADEMY OF DRAMATIC ARTS

External Acting

It is ludicrous to believe that RADA only teaches external acting. To make a point, let's accept this as truth. Do we ignore the power of externals when we are acting? Do we ignore how we react to the clothes we wear, the objects we handle and the environments we live in, or the physicalities learned from working on animals and inanimate objects?

Externals are increasingly important when working on physical traits such as a limp or a speech impediment, on performance styles such as Noel Coward, George Bernard Shaw or Samuel Beckett, or on classical styles such as Greek, Elizabethan or Restoration. All this work only services the growth and eventual marketability of the young actor.

I met with the president of RADA several years ago. He graciously gave me two hours of his time. I learned that RADA teaches many of the same classes we teach in the states. It is important to the RADA graduate to be proficient in all areas of his craft. The well trained actor is able to perform with equal ease contemporary and classical theatre. Most good university training concentrates on these same goals.

ROBERT LEWIS

It's All in the Family

Bobby Lewis honors the craft and all its approaches. In his wonderful book, *Method or Madness*, Bobby Lewis doesn't as much defend the Stanislavsky's system as he clears the air as to its true meaning.

Mr. Lewis believed strongly in using performance concentration and energy in classroom work. "A high A is a high A whether in a rehearsal hall or on the operatic stage."

"The modern acting talent ought to have a line from his head to his heart with the circuits open and the line well traveled in both directions."

Robert Lewis, the thief: "Let me confess," he states, "I have stolen and stolen other teachers' exercises from my Group Theatre days to the present. And many's the time I've seen some spy sitting in the back row of my own workshop surreptitiously writing in a little black book as some pearl is being dropped. 'Please,' I always say, 'be my guest. How do you think I got it?'"

He added, "Anyone can teach you scales and arpeggios at the piano but not everyone is a great or even a good teacher."

He goes on to say in *Method or Madness:*

> *(There are) people who have a normal interest in all theatre techniques. They are curious about it. They are interested in it because it is part of their profession. Or if they did know something about it, they would like to know more and have some point of view towards it – but toward it and not some rumor.*

I had the great pleasure of spending an afternoon with Bobby Lewis. He insisted I call him Bobby and to this day it is difficult for me to think of him with the more formal, Robert. I found him warm and friendly and available. We spoke of the craft of acting and its approaches.

I told him I never used the word *method* I preferred the word *craft*. He understood completely adding that the word *method* had been tossed about and/or analyzed for so long that it had lost much of its credence. He added that Stanislavsky hadn't coined the word *method*. He called his approach "a system."

I saved Bobby Lewis for last. In his wonderful book, *Advice to the*

Players, he writes about the different approaches "...grab what you can. It's all in the family."

* * * * *

It's about the young actor

It is arrogant to presume I can give the attention due to the teachings of the "Great Gurus" in a short article. My intention is simply to inform those of us who need to be awakened to the *necessity of appreciating all the different approaches to the craft of acting.* If we don't, we are doing a disservice to the young actor.

Was Michael Chekhov's debunking of Stanislavsky necessary? Or could he have simply said I have found new approaches to the craft that work well for me? I believe they should be included in the tool kits of our craft. Is this not also true of the teachers today carrying on in the traditions of their teachers? They should also encourage the young actor to explore other acting tools.

A young girl became hysterical when I dared suggest that some other teaching besides the Meisner Technique was valid. Granted, she overreacted, but her overreaction exposed a fear. If I negated her teacher was I negating all the time she spent learning her craft?

All the teachers who entered my life enriched me:

Stella Adler gave me a respect for theatre and craft.

The APA Repertory Company where I found what I felt was missing in my education, "The Strasberg Method" It was here I was also introduced to exercises developed at the Royal Academy of Dramatic Arts.

Michael Howard taught me how to deal with my nerves and introduced me to new exercises.

My teacher Eugenie Leontovich the protégé of Stanislavsky who in her late eighties gave me insight into Stanislavsky and shared with me the expertise she acquired in those years.

Tracey Roberts introduced me to the teachings of Michael Chekhov.

Uta Hagen's books are bibles to myself and to many other actors.

* * * * *

To the Actor: There are many wonderful teachers that have developed wonderful ways of approaching this craft. There are many charlatans out there as well. You do not have to be certified to be an acting teacher. Know with whom you are studying.

Find a teacher who appreciates the many exercises of the past and utilizes them along with their own approach. Look at what was presented in this article and ask yourself if you are proficient in all areas. If not find the teacher who can give you what you need. Don't let anyone tell you that something is not important. If you feel your work is lacking in some area it most likely is.

Teachers have to pay their rent so it is hard to lose a student to another teacher. However, it is about the student. For example, if I see a student has not been able to get out of their head (approaching everything intellectually), I am not above sending that student to a Meisner class.

I recommended one of my students to Sanford Meisner. He was teaching what were to be his last classes. I was pleased to learn he had heard of me and though I didn't teach the Meisner technique exclusively, he approved of my work. By sending my student to another teacher I received one hell of a compliment from one of the Great Gurus.

* * * * *

To the Teacher: To all you teachers who genuinely love your craft and the students who come to you for wisdom, I wish you continued success and growth. Never stand still.

A famous teacher once asked me why I never tired of teaching. She claimed to doze frequently in class. "My answer is simple," I told her. "I never teach the same class twice. I teach the same tools but with a fresh approach. I read constantly and see what new approaches intrigue me and incorporate them into my classes."

"Grab what you can, it's all in the family."

From **The Prophet**

by Khalil Gibran

You work that you may keep peace with the earth and the soul of the earth.

For to be idle is to become a stranger unto the seasons, and to step out of life's procession, that marches in majesty and proud submission toward the infinite.

Work is love made visible.

And if you cannot work with love but only with distaste, it is better that you should leave your work and sit at a gate of the temple and take alms of those who work with joy.

For is you bake a cake with indifference, you bake a bitter bread that feeds but half man's hunger.

And if you grudge the crushing of grapes, your grudge distills a poison in the wine.

And if you sing though as angels, and love not the singing, you muffle man's ears to the voices of the day and the voices of the night.

And what is to work with love?

It is to weave the cloth with threads drawn from your heart, as if your beloved were to wear that cloth.

It is to build a house with affection, as if your beloved were to dwell in that house. It is to sow seeds with tenderness and reap the harvest with joy, as if your beloved were to eat the fruit.

It is to charge that all things you fashion with a breath of your own spirit.

And to know that all blessed dead are standing about you and watching.

Study with Adam Hill

Adam is currently the lead teacher at Craft Acting Studio in Las Vegas, NV. From their website:

CRAFT Acting is the product of many years of study, passion and education. Brad Garrett founded the studio with Adam Hill in the spring of 2013, along with other nationally-renowned coaches in the performing arts. On occasion, courses are taught by Brad Garrett himself, for advanced actors focusing on sitcom work.

The purpose of all classes is to develop a strong work ethic. The classes are designed to teach the full craft of acting enabling the student to be in command of their inherent abilities and to reach their full potential.

Classes and workshops are offered for actors at all ages and all levels. For more information, please visit:

www.Craft-Acting.com

Learn more from Adam and other teaching artists, discover further tools to support your growth, and stay engaged in the Craft-Acting community by connecting with us at:

Facebook: /CraftActing

Twitter: @CraftActing

You Tube: /StageSuccessNetwork (Craft Acting partner)

Tumblr: craftacting.tumblr.com

More from Adam...

You Got the Job! (and what YOU did to get it) – In this companion piece to *Beyond the Moon,* Adam covers the business of acting: approaching your career as a professional, what the industry is looking for, and developing a successful mindset. Written for actors pursuing lasting professional careers.

Stages – Watch Adam speak to groups of actors in this hour-long documentary about succeeding at every stage of a career. In support of his message, meet actors at their unique stages, from just starting in NYC to multi-Emmy Award-winning talent. With examples from the careers of the cast, animation, and more, *Stages* will engage and enlighten any sincere actor who is eager to carve out a career in showbiz.

Learn more at: **www.StagesTheMovie.com**

* * * * *

Michael Schreiber is the editor of the most recent editions of *Beyond the Moon* and *You Got the Job* and the producer of *Stages.* He works extensively with young and beginning actors. Connect with him directly...

on Twitter and Instagram: @schreibrations

Facebook: /schreiber.michael

Made in the USA
San Bernardino, CA
05 February 2015